How to Repair
Plastic
Bodywork

Other Books in the
Whitehorse Press Tech Series

How to Repair
Plastic
Bodywork

Practical, Money-Saving Techniques for Cars,
Motorcycles, Trucks, ATVs, and Snowmobiles

KURT LAMMON

A Tech Series Book
Whitehorse Press
North Conway, New Hampshire

Cover photo by Scott Bixler

We recognize that some words, model names, and designations mentioned herein are the property of the trademark holder. We use them for identification purposes only.

Whitehorse Press is a trademark of Kennedy Associates.

Whitehorse Press books are also available at discounts in bulk quantity for sales and promotional use. For details about special sales or for a catalog of motorcycling books and videos, write to the publisher:

Whitehorse Press
P.O. Box 60
North Conway, New Hampshire 03860-0060
Phone: 603-356-6556 or 800-531-1133
E-mail: Orders@WhitehorsePress.com
Internet: www.WhitehorsePress.com

ISBN 1-884313-37-X

5 4 3 2 1

Printed in Hong Kong

Contents

Introduction

Since the mid-70s, the use of plastics in automobiles, motorcycles, and other vehicles has expanded exponentially. In 1970, the average automobile had 70 pounds of plastic material. In 2000, plastics usage had increased to some 260 pounds per vehicle. Motorcycles have used plastic body panels for more than two decades with many modern bikes nearly completely covered in plastic. Now the same technology is being used to produce vertical body panels on automobiles such as the Volkswagen Beetle, the Saturn, and Europe's Smart car.

This trend toward increased plastic usage is not going to stop anytime soon. To give you an idea of where the innovation is heading, DaimlerChrysler has already constructed a prototype car for which the chassis—not just the body panels, but the entire load-bearing structure—is molded entirely of recycled soda bottles. Desire by original equipment manufacturers (OEMs) for reduced costs, parts consolidation, weight reduction, recyclablity, environmental friendliness, and design flexibility will continue to drive greater innovation in plastic materials in the future, ensuring ever-expanding usage of plastic in vehicles of every type.

One thing that's not likely to change is the economics of plastic molding. As long as only one company owns the mold to make the part, the replacement part will be expensive. The cost of the plastic resin in a one-pound motorcycle side fairing is approximately 85 cents, but anyone who's crashed his bike knows that they're charging more than that for a replacement part!

Because plastics usage will continue to increase and the cost of plastic parts will probably not come down, it makes good sense for the repair technician and even the do-it-yourselfer to learn how to repair plastics. All of today's plastic repair technologies are designed to be easy to use. However, because there is no universal re-

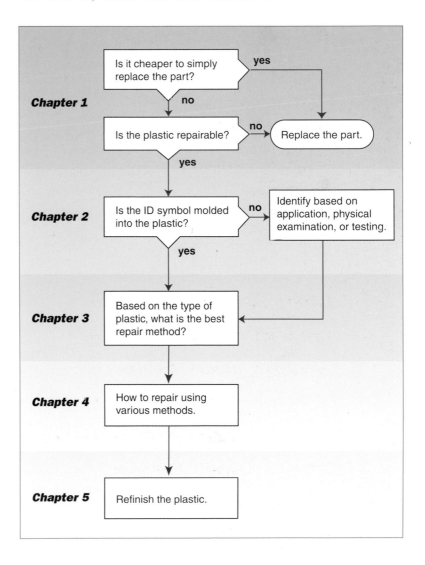

pair method that will repair all plastics, the biggest problem in plastic repair is not the repair materials themselves but technician education. That is the purpose of this book.

The first step of any plastic repair project is to decide whether or not to do the repair in the first place. Sometimes aftermarket copies of certain plastic parts are available. As a result, often the OEM will reduce the price to compete with the knockoff. If this is the case, it may be a better use of your time to throw away the broken part and replace it. I'll talk about some of the repair vs. replace issues in the first chapter of this book.

Let's assume you decide to repair the broken part. In order to decide on a suitable repair method, you must first identify the plastic; the second chapter of this book will show you how to do that. The simplest way is to find the plastic ID symbol that is often molded into the backside of the part somewhere. If you can't find the ID symbol, I'll discuss some ways to distinguish between types of plastic in general, and also talk about specific types of plastic used in popular applications.

Once the plastic has been identified, the third chapter of the book will discuss repair options for each type of plastic, as well as the pros and cons of each. Some types of plastic may only be repairable by one method; other types can be repaired by many different methods. The choice you make for the repair will probably depend more on the tools you have in your toolbox. For example, some repair technologies, such as hot-air welding, will not be as accessible to the do-it-yourselfer. Of course, I'll give you detailed instructions for each different method.

Naturally, after you finish your repair, you will want it to look like new again. Some plastics are simple to paint; others are impossible. I'll let you know the best way to refinish each type of plastic. The final chapter of the book is devoted to this subject.

The basic structure of the book is laid out in the following graphic. The book is designed to be easy to navigate for the simple repair job, yet detailed enough to act as a textbook for a thorough understanding of the subject. I've put the highly detailed and technical material in the appendices so as to not slow down the reader who simply wants to *use* an adhesive and doesn't really care *how* it works.

To Repair or Not to Repair . . .
That's the First Question

Most plastic parts on cars and motorcycles are not stressed components, so if a part breaks, it's most likely the result of an accident. For example, somebody backs into your car in the parking lot and cracks your bumper; or your motorcycle falls off the centerstand and breaks the plastic side panel. It was an accident, but for whatever reason, you've got yourself a broken piece of plastic.

The first question you need to ask is, "Do I need to repair this at all?" Maybe you've got a deep gouge in your plastic bumper, but it's a twelve-year-old car with 200,000 miles on it. You can probably live with that. Or maybe you've got an older dirt bike and one of the three pins that holds on the sidecover breaks off. If it hangs on okay with the other two pins, you may be able to live with that. The point is, if the plastic part still performs to your expectations even after it's broken, then there's probably no need to spend the time or money to repair or replace it.

I assume, however, since you're reading this book, you've got a plastic part that's damaged enough to render it unserviceable, or at least unsightly. The next question to ask is, "Can I repair this part, or should it be replaced?"

The answer to this question totally depends on the price of the replacement part. Usually it's the case that the part is more expensive than you think it should be. "What?! $450 for a stinkin' piece of plastic! Outrageous!"

The price of replacement parts are affected by the costs of packaging, warehousing, and distributing the parts and these costs are not trivial. For example, the ability to walk into a Yamaha dealer and get a brand new sidecover for a 1985 FZ750, all nicely boxed and bubble wrapped, does not come for nothing. You don't think about the fact that the part was probably molded in Japan three years ago, painted and decorated, packaged, and shipped to the United States, where it sat on a shelf in some warehouse in California until your dealer finally called up and ordered it. These inventory carrying costs will naturally be passed along to the consumer.

Cost to Repair $<$ Cost to Replace

Cost to Repair		Cost to Replace
● Repair Labor Cost	$<$	● Replacement Part Cost
● Repair Material Cost		● Refinishing Labor Cost
● Refinishing Labor Cost		● Refinishing Material Cost
● Refinishing Material Cost		● Removal/Installation Labor
● Removal/Installation Labor Cost		Cost
● (Cost to re-do repair if faulty) x (probability of faulty repair)		

Factors to consider:

- Repairs can sometimes be done in place, eliminating the requirement to remove and reinstall the part.
- Spot repairs can save refinishing material and labor cost since entire part does not have to be refinished.
- Adhesion of refinish coat can be better on repaired OEM part as opposed to aftermarket replacement part.
- Availability of replacement part; if not readily available, may tilt decision toward repair.
- Fit and finish of aftermarket replacement part, if used.
- Confidence in doing repair vs. cost and damage to reputation to re-do faulty repair.

But the main reason why replacement parts are so expensive is because there is usually only one company that owns the tooling to mold the part. If the manufacturer has a monopoly on the supply of the part, he can charge whatever the market will bear.

To some extent, the high prices for replacement parts are justified to pay back the investment the company made to create the mold. These molds can be incredibly expensive. Depending on the size and shape of the part, the mold could cost anywhere from $25,000 for a small, simple part to $500,000 for a large, complex bumper fascia mold.

There are several reasons for the high cost of these molds. Molds for injection molded thermoplastics are precision machined from blocks of solid steel, and the larger the part, the larger the piece of steel has to be. The machine tools and CAD systems used to design and create the molds are also very expensive, and their costs must be amortized into the cost of the mold. These molds are often hand-finished and polished, which requires skilled labor. Finally, a lot of expensive engineering talent goes into designing the mold and making sure the plastic flows into it properly to minimize manufacturing defects and scrap.

There are a few cases where there is enough of a demand for replacement plastic parts that it entices another manufacturer to create his own mold and sell an aftermarket alternative to the OEM part. A good example are the *crash parts* on popular cars, typically front end parts like bumper fascia, grilles, and headlights. There are a few North American and several Taiwanese aftermarket manufacturers of automotive plastic crash parts that do very well supplying the need for OEM alternatives.

Many people gripe that the quality of the aftermarket parts aren't up to the standards of the original OEM parts. Although this is sometimes true, it is also true that it is always a benefit to the consumer when the aftermarkets come out because the OEM will usually decrease its price to be more competitive. An OEM front bumper cover that originally sold for $400 might drop to $200 when an aftermarket part becomes available.

It may be, that for a popular, high-volume car like a Honda Civic, there are three different aftermarket manufacturers for the front bumper fascia, dropping the street price for a bumper to

Injection Molding: How It Works

The process of thermoplastic injection molding involves the rapid pressure filling of a closed mold cavity with a molten charge of plastic. The injection molding machine is filled with a supply of solid plastic pellets. These pellets are fed into an extruder/plunger that heats the pellets to the melting temperature and homogenizes the mixture. When the mold is ready, the plunger injects a set amount of the molten plastic into the mold at very high pressure (10,000 to 30,000 psi). The mold is cooled to a temperature below that of the solidification temperature of the plastic, so, over a short period of time, the plastic cools and solidifies sufficiently for it to be removed from the mold. Once the part is ejected from the mold, the cycle is repeated.

Due to the high pressures involved, the molds must be machined from thick blocks of stainless steel. If the part features undercuts or re-entrant shapes, as they often do, the mold becomes much more complicated by the addition of retractable secondary mold sections. The molds will also feature movable pins to push the finished part out of the mold and cooling passages throughout to keep it at the proper temperature. ∎

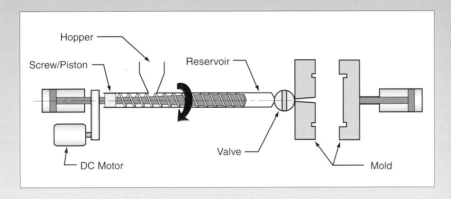

Plastication Stage
Extruder fills reservoir with melted plastic charge.

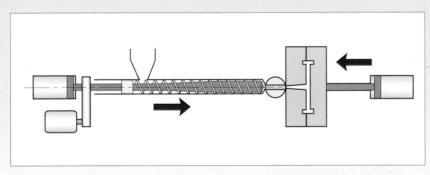

Injection Stage
Mold closes, valve opens, and injection machine screw/piston moves forward to inject melted plastic charge into mold. High pressure is exerted by the piston (10,000–30,000 psi) to rapidly complete filling of the mold and to minimize shrinkage of the material upon cooling.

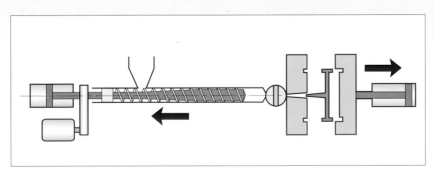

Ejection Stage
Valve closes, screw/piston retracts to begin plastication for next injection shot. Once molded part has solidified sufficiently, the mold retracts and the finished part is demolded. Machine is ready for next cycle.

around $80. At this price level, it almost makes no sense to spend any time repairing the bumper. For anything bigger than a simple gouge, you'd be better off throwing the bumper away and installing an aftermarket part, especially if the bumper has an unpainted, textured finish. However, if the bumper has no aftermarket competition, its price could range from $300 to $600, and sometimes as high as $1,500. At this price level, it could be worth your while to spend a few hours repairing it.

So, how do you know when to repair and when to replace? Simply put, if the cost to repair the part is less than the cost to replace it, then repair the part. Realize, however, that there are a lot of factors involved that require some experience in doing plastic repairs to determine.

If you are reading this book for the first time, you probably don't have the experience necessary to answer all of these questions in detail. Most of the time you won't have to—the economics of the situation are usually very obvious. For example, replacement parts for street bikes are usually so ridiculously expensive that it makes good sense to try to repair them even if you're not sure of all the costs involved.

Easier	More Difficult
Crack in flat area with plenty of area surrounding it.	Crack near edge, also has stylistic feature running through it.
Tab is in same plane as part.	Tab is perpendicular to the plane of the part.

Three Factors to Consider

When considering whether to repair or replace a part, three factors come to the forefront: the composition of the plastic, the geometry of the damaged area and the amount of surface area surrounding it, and the ease with which the plastic can be refinished.

Some plastics are easier to repair than others. Rigid plastics tend to be easier to repair, mainly because adhesives stick to them more easily. There are usually a greater number of repair options available for the repair of rigid plastics, making it more likely that one repair option will be ideally suited to the type of damage that needs to be repaired. On the other hand, some types of plastic, such as the low-density polyethylene commonly used on dirt bikes and ATVs, are more difficult to repair because adhesives don't stick to them very well at all. Welding is often the only viable repair option for these types of plastic.

The geometry of the damaged area and the amount of surface area surrounding it is important because most plastic repair technologies are adhesive based. The strength of an adhesive repair typically rises in direct proportion to the amount of area over which the adhesive is spread. In other words, the greater the area over which you can spread the adhesive, the stronger the repair will be.

Generally, the more open area there is around the damage, the easier it will be to repair. It also helps immensely if the backside of the part is non-cosmetic, allowing a reinforcing buildup. Conversely, if there is a lot of detail in the area that needs to be preserved, or if the piece that has broken off protrudes at right angles to the part, the part may be very difficult or impossible to repair. Table 1.1 also gives some rules of thumb regarding the ease of doing a repair based on surface area/geometry considerations.

Of course, it would be impossible to exhaustively list all of the considerations that could come into play with respect to repairability, but this should give you some guidelines to go by. After you gain some experience with a few of the different repair methods, you should have a much better idea of what is doable and what is not.

Refinishing

The final factor to consider in whether a part should be repaired or replaced is the ease with which the part can be refinished. Plastic parts come either in their raw state or painted. Cosmetic plastic parts can be painted, as most car bumpers or motorcycle fairings are, or they can be molded in color, as ATV fenders are. Most non-cosmetic plastic parts are not painted, as this additional manufacturing step would be a waste of money.

Cosmetic parts tend to be more expensive, especially if they are painted or decorated with decals. Fortunately, it is actually easier to refinish parts if they are painted. The original finish can be sanded off, the repair area filled with a sandable filler material, then a fresh coat of paint can be applied to cover everything up.

Refinishing is much more difficult in the case of an unpainted cosmetic part. Often these parts are *textured*. If you look closely at the surface of such a part, they are usually not smooth; rather they have a small, even pattern of dots or perhaps a leather grain over the whole surface. This is especially common on trim pieces like door handles, mirrors, and rub strips. Often, entire bumper covers are made this way. Making things more difficult is the fact that these parts are usually molded from thermoplastic olefinic (TPO) plastics, which are difficult to get paint to adhere to.

These types of plastic are quite easy to repair, as we shall see, but they are hard to refinish. As of this writing, there is no technology available that can duplicate the uniform pattern on the surface of these parts. You can simulate the surface appearance by spraying on a texture coating, but it is hard to blend the sprayed texture into the original. This usually necessitates sanding off all of the original texture by hand, then retexturing the entire part. After the part has been retextured, it then has to be painted in a matching color.

All of the time and money spent sanding and painting these parts has to be compared to the cost of a new replacement part. Remember, textured, unfinished parts are usually less expensive than their painted counterparts, thus lowering the replacement threshold.

Table 1.1 - Ease of Repair Rules of Thumb	
Repair Is Easier If . . .	**Repair Is More Difficult If . . .**
Crack is in the middle of an open, flat area.	Crack is in a corner or close to edge.
Backside of the part is accessible for repair.	Backside of part is inaccessible for repair, as it would be for a fuel or water tank.
Backside of part is hidden, allowing for a buildup of reinforcing material.	Backside of part is visible and needs to have original appearance.
There exists clearance between the part and adjoining hardware to allow for a buildup of reinforcing material on the backside.	Adjoining hardware fits tightly against the backside of the part, not allowing for a buildup of reinforcing material on the backside.
Protruding piece breaks taking the base with it, increasing the surface area available for making the repair.	Protruding piece breaks off right at base, leaving very little surface area available for making the repair.
Part is meltable plastic (thermoplastic).	Part is not meltable (thermoset).

ATV and dirt bike fenders are another common example of a difficult-to-refinish part. These parts are usually made from polyethylene, like TPO, an olefinic plastic that feels "oily" to the touch. This characteristic makes it hard for mud and dirt to stick to it, so it's easy to wash off all the crud with a stream of high-pressure water. In addition, polyethylene is tough, flexible, cheap, and extremely resistant to chemical attack, making it great for gas tanks and such.

This oily, chemical-resistant nature of polyethylene also makes it nearly impossible for paint to stick to it. Polyethylene is actually quite easy to repair using plastic welding techniques, as we'll see later in this book, but because polyethylene is virtually impossible to refinish, parts made from this material tend to be replaced rather than repaired.

This brings us back to one of the first points brought up in this chapter regarding your expectation for the appearance of the part. Say you've got an older dirt bike. You're not so concerned about the appearance of the repair. You can easily do a weld repair that that will restore the function of the part. In fact, the repair can be reinforced to provide greater strength than the original. However, because polyethylene is impossible to refinish, you won't be able to sand, fill, and paint the repair area, so the repair will be visible. This might be fine if you have an older bike, or if you simply can't find a replacement part. However, if you have a new, clean bike, the appearance of the repaired part might not be acceptable to you, driving you to replace it.

Hopefully you now have some insights about the factors involved in deciding whether to replace or repair a broken plastic part. You probably won't gain a "seat-of-the-pants" feel for repairablity until you've actually done some repairs, so it's best to try your hand on some expensive parts that you'd have to replace anyway.

CHAPTER 2

Identifying the Type of Plastic

Previous epochs of human development have been labeled according to the types of materials used at the time—witness the Stone Age, Iron Age, and the Bronze Age. By the same logic, the 20th century could certainly be labeled the Plastics Age. The plastics age was born in the late 19th century when entrepreneurs began looking for a material other than ivory from which to make billiard balls. The development of plastics has since expanded at an exponential pace. Today there are about 50 distinct generic types of plastic materials for material designers to choose from. Over 250 plastic resin manufacturers worldwide sell more than 20,000 commercial brands of plastic.

Fortunately for the repair technician, there are only a few generic types of plastic that are commonly used, and we don't need to be too concerned with the small differences between the different commercial brands. This chapter will introduce the major generic types of plastic and the process for telling one from another.

Why Do We Need to Identify the Plastic?

Some manufacturers of plastic repair adhesives claim that the plastic does not need to be identified in order to use their product. Generally these manufacturers classify plastics as either *rigid* or *flexible* and provide different materials to repair each type.

This simplified approach works in most cases and solves an important problem: the reluctance of a technician to attempt a repair due to his perceived difficulty of the process. Because identifying the plastic is usually the most difficult part

of the repair process, boiling this step down to rigid or flexible enables people to attempt repairs which they might have otherwise thought were too difficult.

The only drawback is that it locks you into one plastic repair process, which may not work in every instance. By identifying the plastic, you are better able to identify the best repair methods. A good example is the repair of polyethylene. It could be classified as a flexible or semi-rigid plastic, depending on the geometry of the part. However, most adhesives will not stick to polyethylene, regardless. By identifying the ma-

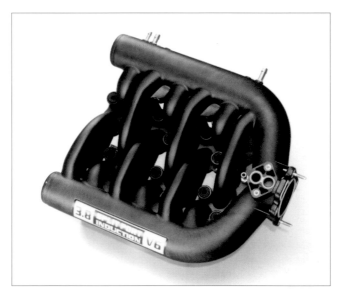

Not too many years ago, it would have been unthinkable to make an intake manifold from plastic, because of high engine temperatures. Material and injection molding technology have now combined to offer the flexibility of intricate shapes and low manufacturing cost.

What Is a Polymer?

At the molecular level, all of the materials commonly known as *plastics* are made of long chains of carbon-based building block molecules called monomers. A monomer is a small molecule that has the inherent capability of forming chemical bonds with the same or other monomers in such a way that long chains, called polymers (meaning "many monomers"), are formed. The properties of the resultant plastic material depend on the combination of monomers in the chains, the length of the chains, any branching that occurs off the chains, or any crosslinking that occurs between chains.

The word "long" is a relative term. Compared to the size of other organic or inorganic molecules, polymer chains are long. The polymer chains normally consist of between 100 and 10,000 monomer building blocks. The actual length of a polymer chain consisting of 1000 monomers would be about 0.0003 mm, or about one-third the diameter of a human hair. Even the longest polymer chains, those of ultra-high-molecular-weight polyethylene (about 200,000 building blocks long), would only be about 0.06 mm long.

These polymer chains may be randomly oriented (amorphous, like a bundle of snakes) or, in some types of plastics, they may achieve an ordered crystalline formation. The physical properties of the plastic depend on this as well. Amorphous plastics soften at a temperature called the *glass transition temperature*. Depending on their level of crystallinity, crystalline plastics will soften slightly at a glass transition temperature, but will remain solid (or semi-crystalline) up to the melt transition temperature or melting point. Crystalline plastics tend to soften and melt at higher temperatures than do amorphous plastics.

The following table shows the monomer structure of various common thermoplastics and their transition temperatures. They are listed in order of increasing melting or softening point. ∎

Table 2.1 Monomer Structures and Melting Points of Various Polymers				
Plastic	**Monomer Structure**	**Crystalline?**	**Glass Transistion Temp (deg. F)**	**Melting Point (deg. F)**
PVC		NO	158	n/a
PS - polystyrene		NO	212	n/a
PMMA - acrylic		NO	221	n/a
PE - polyethylene		YES	− 148	248
PP - polypropylene		YES	− 4	347
PA-6 - nylon		YES	122	428
PC - polycarbonate		YES	302	446
PET		YES	158	509

terial, you would probably decide to weld the plastic, which would be the best repair method. In this book, I'll do my best to simplify the identification process to some basic rules of thumb. For most commonly damaged parts on vehicles and recreational equipment, identification is very straightforward.

Thermoplastics vs. Thermosets

All of the 50-plus generic plastic types fall into one of two broad categories of plastics that relate to their basic chemical composition: *thermoplastics* and *thermosets*.

Thermoplastics make up the vast majority of the generic types of plastic and are the ones that are most commonly used on vehicles, recreational equipment, and household products. Thermoplastics are composed of long carbon molecule chains that can slide past one another when heated. When heated to a certain point, the material can flow, and when cooled, it becomes solid again.

Think of a pot of spaghetti and cheese sauce. When cool, the spaghetti and cheese form a solid block of material. Put it on the stove, melt the cheese sauce, and the strands of spaghetti can flow past one another, allowing you to pour it out onto a plate. When it cools off, it forms a solid block again. You can repeat this process by heating it up again.

Thermoset plastics are different only in one way: the carbon molecule chains form *crosslinks* with other nearby carbon molecule chains. This simple difference completely changes the character of the plastic, however. To process it, the plastic must be *cast in place*. Usually two components are mixed together and poured or injected into the mold. After the polymerizing reaction takes place, the part cannot be reverted back to its constituents again. Applying heat and pressure will not cause a thermoset plastic to flow or deform. Excessive heat will simply destroy the plastic altogether.

In this respect, thermosets are like concrete. First, you dig the hole or otherwise prepare the "mold." You then combine the ready-mix with water and gravel, and pour the mixture into the mold. Give it some time to set up and it's *set*. There's nothing you can do to break it back down

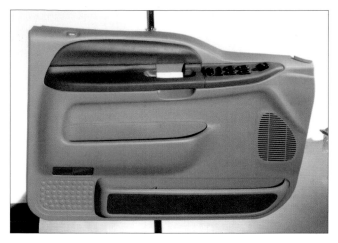

Highly complex shapes, such as the parts used in this inner door panel, are quite practical when proper materials and manufacturing methods are used.

into ready-mix and water. You've created a new material.

An easy way to remember the difference between *thermoplastic* and *thermoset* is to think of the fact that a thermo*set* is *set*, like concrete, and it can't be molded or deformed with heat or pressure. A thermo*plastic*, on the other hand, is *plastic;* in other words, it can be deformed with heat and pressure.

Thermoplastics: The Most Common Class of Plastic Material

Thermoplastics are the most common type of plastic material used on vehicles, recreational equipment, and household products. Most of the products you think of as "plastic" are made of thermoplastics—plastic bags, vinyl seat covers, computer cases, and children's toys, just to name a few. Here are some of the most common types of thermoplastic materials and some of their common applications:

Polypropylene splash guards, inner fender liners, body side molding, bumper covers

Polyethylene battery cases, water tanks, ATV and dirt bike fenders, household items

Acrylonitrile Butadiene Styrene (ABS) motorcycle fairings, interior plastics, trim panels, computer cases

Polycarbonate plastic windows, automotive body panels, bumpers, household items

Nylon (Polyamide) radiator tanks, intake manifolds, pipe, rope

Polyvinyl Chloride (PVC) pipe, seat covers, architectural products

A manufacturer of such thermoplastic products will buy the plastic resin in pelletized form from a resin manufacturer. There are more than 200 such manufacturers worldwide, examples being GE Plastics and Dow Chemical. These pellets are fed into a machine that heats the pellets and makes them flow under pressure. Once "melted," the plastic is molded or formed into its final shape by a variety of processes. The plastic is then cooled until it resolidifies, at which point it is ready for use or further processing.

For the most part, thermoplastics are best suited for mass production. Because the cost of the equipment required to mold or process thermoplastics is so high, using thermoplastics doesn't make good economic sense unless you can spread the up-front costs over a lot of product. For example, the cost of the mold or tool used to create a plastic bumper cover may be in the range of $500,000, so the manufacturer will need to ensure that there's going to be enough volume to recover the tooling cost.

Thermosets: Better Suited to Low-Volume Manufacturing or Large Parts

Despite the prevalence of thermoplastics, products made from thermoset resins are still extremely common, especially on lower-volume or very large parts. The main advantage of thermoset resins is that they can be processed on lower-cost tooling, making them better suited to one-offs and small production runs. Thermoset resins are ideal for large parts like boat hulls where high tooling costs and the limitations of injection molding prohibit the use of thermoplastic resins.

Thermoset plastics are usually created via a chemical reaction between two liquid components. Some time after the components are mixed, the crosslinking reaction occurs, creating the plastic. Depending on the type of resin, this crosslinking reaction may also be catalyzed by moisture in the air or by heat. In any case, as a result of the crosslinks that form between the molecular chains, the structure of the resulting material is different than that of either of the components. As a result, after the crosslinking reaction takes place, the application of heat or pressure to the material will not cause it to break down into its original components.

The following are examples of some very common thermosetting resins:

Epoxy adhesives and fillers, fiberglass, and carbon-fiber composites

Urethane adhesives, car bumpers, fenders, truck beds

Polyester fiberglass boat hulls, Sheet Molding Composite (SMC) body panels, automotive body filler

When parts made from thermosetting resins are used as structural components, they are most often reinforced with mineral fillers or glass strands. Popular terms such as *fiberglass* or *carbon fiber* actually refer to composite structures of these fiber reinforcements and a surrounding layer of either an epoxy or polyester thermoset resin.

Table 2.1 shows the most common generic types of plastic materials used on vehicles, recreation equipment, and household products. The

Table 2.2 - Common Bumper Fascia Plastics		
Plastic Type	**ID Symbols**	**ID Tips**
Polyurethane (Thermoset)	PUR, RIM, RRIM	Color may be yellow or gray. Bumper covers are quite flexible; fenders and other body parts may be quite rigid. Heavier than water. Will bubble and smoke if overheated with welder.
Thermoplastic Olefin	TPO, TEO, PP+EPDM	Color is usually black or gray with a shiny, greasy appearance. It is more rigid than urethane bumpers, less rigid than Xenoy, and melts and smears when ground. Lighter than water. Melts and resolidifies when heated with welder.
Xenoy (Thermoplastic)	PC+PBT	Very rigid. Usually molded in dark color, but may be molded in any color. Heavier than water. Melts and resolidifies when heated with welder.

Thermoplastic Manufacturing Processes

There are about a dozen different manufacturing processes for making products from thermoplastics. Most of the parts on cars and motorcycles will be injection molded, but you'll occasionally see sheet thermoformed or rotationally molded parts as well. The mother of all manufacturing processes, and the basis of most of them, is extrusion.

Extrusion The basic process of extrusion works like this: Thermoplastic pellets are first poured into a hopper in the extrusion machine. At the bottom of the hopper is a screw (or screws) that feeds the pellets into a heated barrel. The heat from the barrel and the friction caused by the turning screw will cause the pellets to melt as they pass through the barrel. When the plastic

Thermoplastic extrusion machine

exits the end of the barrel, it comes out mixed and melted, ready for further processing.

The melted extrudate may be fed through tools to create profiles like pipe, be flattened into sheets, or blown to make plastic bags. Just about all thermoplastic manufacturing processes depend on extrusion as the heart of the process.

Injection Molding Injection molding machines have an extrusion screw that doubles as an injection piston. The extrusion screw turns to fill up a cavity just upstream of the mold with melted plastic. At the proper time, the screw itself, doubling as a piston, drives forward, pushing the proper amount of melted plastic into the mold under high pressure. While the injected material is cooling and solidifying, the extrusion screw/piston retracts and turns again to fill the chamber with more melted plastic, preparing for the next charge.

The mold is cooled, so it extracts heat from the melted plastic, allowing it to solidify. After a certain amount of time (usually on the order of seconds), the mold opens and the part is ejected. The mold closes for the cycle to be repeated again.

Thermoforming The thermoforming process creates shapes by heating and softening thermoplastic sheet stock (itself created by an extrusion process) and forcing it by vacuum or pressure into a single-sided mold. This process is not commonly used on vehicular applications, but it can be used to create

(cont. on next page)

Thermoforming Process

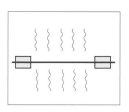

Heating Sheet stock is clamped in a frame that is shaped to fit the mold. The sheet is then heated in an oven until it softens.

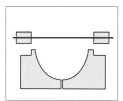

Positioning The softened blank and clamp frame is placed onto the tool (mold).

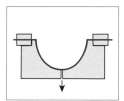

Forming Air is withdrawn from inside the tool, allowing atmospheric pressure to force the softened blank into the mold, where it conforms to the mold dimensions.

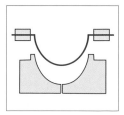

Unloading The plastic cools upon contact with the mold. Once it achieves sufficient rigidity, the frame can be withdrawn. The formed part is then removed from the clamp frame for trimming and further processing.

hollow shapes such as tanks. Thermoformed parts are characterized by a smooth surface finish on both sides and have a flange that lies in a single plane (unless the flange has been trimmed off). Thermoforming has been used with great success to form large pieces, such as personal watercraft hulls and farm tractor fenders.

Rotational Molding   Rotational molding is used to make hollow products, particularly fluid storage tanks. The process works by introducing a powdered thermoplastic charge into a clamshell-like mold, then heating and tumbling the mold simultaneously. Rotationally molded parts are characterized by a slightly rough outer surface. Most rotationally molded parts used on vehicular applications, such as radiator overflow tanks and windshield washer bottles, are made of high-density polyethylene. Some small, hollow parts may also be formed by blow-molding. ∎

Rotational Molding

Loading
A finely powdered thermoplastic charge is placed in the mold. The mold is closed and clamped shut.

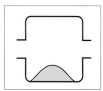

Heating
The mold is placed in a machine that tumbles it about two axes. The mold is simultaneously heated. The thermoplastic charge is melted as it comes into contact with the heated mold walls during the tumbling process.

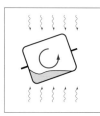

Cooling
As the mold continues to tumble, it is subjected to rapid cooling, causing solidification of the part.

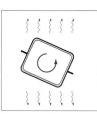

Unloading
Once the part is sufficiently solidified, the mold is unclamped and the finished part is ejected.

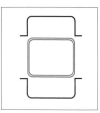

ABS motorcycle side cover

table shows the ID symbol, typical applications, identification tips, and the recommended repair procedure for each type.

In the rest of this chapter, I'll focus individually on the plastics typically found on automobiles, motorcycles, and recreational equipment, which is what you're probably most interested in repairing.

Identifying Automotive Plastics

The use of plastics on cars and trucks has been expanding so rapidly that any book on the subject is likely to appear outdated in a short time. In 30 years, the technology has moved from molding simple door panels and consoles from ABS to complete cars being made from injection-molded thermoplastic. In this book, I'll provide a snapshot of the technology of the early 2000s and a glimpse at technologies likely to become commonplace before the end of the decade.

Bumper Fascia

Plastic bumper fascias began to replace steel automobile bumpers in the late '70s and are now so prevalent that it's nearly impossible to find a late-model car or truck with exposed metal bumpers. There are several reasons why the OEMs switched from metal to plastic: lower cost, greater styling flexibility, and lighter weight.

There are three major families of plastics that are used on automobile and truck bumper fascias: thermoset polyurethane, thermoplastic olefin, and Xenoy (see Table 2.2). These three plastic types cover about 99 percent of the plastic bumpers used on vehicles since the early 1980s.

Xenoy Mercedes bumper

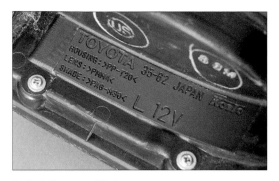

PMMA Toyota taillight

There are a few oddballs out there, and I'll discuss options for repairing them, but I'll just focus on the three dominant types at this point.

Polyurethane was introduced in the mid 1970s as the first flexible material for bumper fascia applications. When federal safety regulations mandated energy-absorbing bumper systems for the first time, manufacturers initially resorted to energy-absorbing mounts for steel bumpers. Sticking out from the car bodies by a foot, those bumpers weren't very appealing aesthetically, so efforts were made to hide the energy-absorbing components behind a flexible plastic cover that was more integrated with the car's bodywork. The Chevrolet Corvette and Camaro are early examples of that new type of construction. Both of these cars were designed in the era of the metal bumper and were retrofitted with urethane covers when the federal mandates came into effect.

As the manufacturers became more accustomed to working with this new material, more and more cars were designed with flexible urethane bumper fascia in mind. Urethane bumper fascia offered much more styling freedom than chromed steel bumpers and the manufacturers took advantage of that to create more appealing designs. Consumers slowly got used to the idea of cars not having chrome bumpers and began to prefer the more integrated look that urethane covers offered.

Thermoset polyurethane has a couple of drawbacks that caused the OEMs to explore other options for bumper fascia material. First of all, polyurethane resin is fairly expensive and is more messy and difficult to process than thermo-

GTX Saturn fender

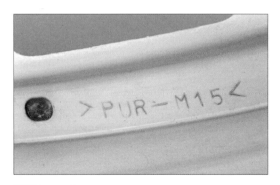

PUR Lexus bumper

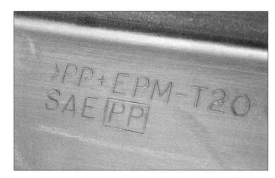

TPO Nissan bumper

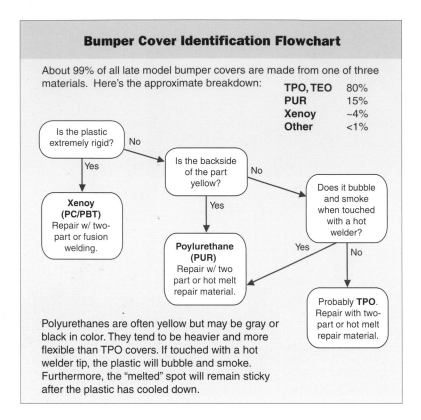

Bumper Cover Identification Flowchart

About 99% of all late model bumper covers are made from one of three materials. Here's the approximate breakdown:

TPO, TEO	80%
PUR	15%
Xenoy	~4%
Other	<1%

Is the plastic extremely rigid?

No → Is the backside of the part yellow?

Yes ↓

Xenoy (PC/PBT)
Repair w/ two-part or fusion welding.

No → Does it bubble and smoke when touched with a hot welder?

Yes ↓

Poylurethane (PUR)
Repair w/ two part or hot melt repair material.

Yes →

No ↓

Probably **TPO**. Repair with two-part or hot melt repair material.

Polyurethanes are often yellow but may be gray or black in color. They tend to be heavier and more flexible than TPO covers. If touched with a hot welder tip, the plastic will bubble and smoke. Furthermore, the "melted" spot will remain sticky after the plastic has cooled down.

plastic resins. More important, however, is the fact that thermoset urethanes cannot be directly recycled.

With thermoplastic injection molding, if there is a problem in the manufacturing process and the mold doesn't fill up completely, for example, the part can be chipped up, put back into the injection molding machine, and re-injected. Defective thermoset urethane parts, however, have to be thrown away; because it can't be broken down into its chemical components again, there's no way to recycle thermoset plastic.

These disadvantages spurred OEMs to search for cheaper, recyclable materials. Beginning in the mid 1980s, some manufacturers, mainly Japanese, began working with polypropylene-based TPO materials. This resin was recyclable and cheaper than thermoset urethane resin. Initially, TPOs were used only on lower-end vehicles where the bumper covers were left unpainted, because TPOs at the time were more difficult to paint than urethane covers. Over the years, improvements and processing modifications have greatly improved paint adhesion on TPO. Now, it is very common to see luxury brands

(marques), such as Lexus and Mercedes Benz, sporting TPO bumper fascias.

The third most common bumper fascia material is Xenoy (pronounced *ZEE-noy*), which is a GE Plastics trade name for their polycarbonate-polyester thermoplastic blend. Ford and GE Plastics worked together extensively for the introduction of the material on the first generation of the Ford Taurus (1986). Xenoy, unlike PUR and TPO, offers great structural strength, and Ford took advantage of this property by consolidating the outer bumper fascia with the underlying bumper reinforcement. The entire fascia/reinforcement assembly bolts up to energy absorbing shocks, just like a steel bumper would. By contrast, PUR and TPO fascia are basically cosmetic covers over steel or plastic energy-absorption structures.

For a period of more than ten years, Ford used Xenoy on several other applications including their Aerostar minivan and Escort line of small cars. European marques, such as Mercedes Benz and BMW, also used it on some applications. Throughout the '80s and '90s, however, great strides were made with the processability and paintability of TPOs, so when Ford introduced the third-generation Taurus in 1996, they used an "industry standard" non-structural TPO fascia over an underlying reinforcement. Xenoy is now rarely used as a cosmetic bumper material, but it is still used and gaining ground as a metal replacement for bumper reinforcements and other underhood and interior applications.

At the time of this writing, approximately 75 to 80 percent of bumper fascia are made from TPO with the balance thermoset polyurethane and a very small amount of Xenoy. Polyurethanes persist for a couple of reasons. First, because the material is injected at lower pressures than thermoplastics are, the production tooling can be made less expensively. This helps when the production volume of the vehicle is smaller, say on a luxury or high-end car. Also, the painted surface finish and paint adhesion to urethane is still better than TPO, which also lends itself to high-end car applications.

Fortunately, these three major bumper fascia plastics are easy to distinguish from each other. First, check the rigidity of the plastic. If it's very

Thermoset vs. Thermoplastic Manufacturing

The manufacture of thermoplastic products is accomplished by heating plastic pellets to a certain processing temperature (at or above the melting point), manipulating or forming the melted plastic into its final shape, and finally allowing the plastic to cool and harden. The process of melting the

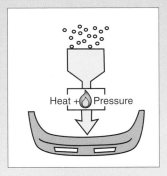

Thermoplastic Molding Process

Thermoset Molding Process

pellets is usually done with an extruder. There are a variety of ways to manipulate and form the melted plastic, including profile extrusion or injection molding. Thermoplastics do not undergo any chemical changes during processing. They simply melt and resolidify.

Thermoset plastics, by contrast, do undergo a chemical change during the manufacturing process. Two liquid or paste-like components are mixed and, while still in a liquid state, are formed into their final shape

by casting, injection molding, or by some other means. The material is held in the forming tool until the chemical reaction that creates the solid material is completed, at which point the finished product is ejected from the mold. Once the chemical reaction between the components is complete, the material cannot be broken back into its constituent components again.

To contrast the process of injection molding in particular, thermoplastic injection molding must be done at much higher pressures. The mold must be designed to withstand the high pressure, and as a result, its cost is driven quite high. Thermosets are usually injected at much lower pressures, and as a result, the tool can be made more cheaply.

Conversely, the resin cost for thermoplastics is cheaper than for thermosets. Also, thermoplastics can be easily recycled. Any scrap from the manufacturing process can be chipped up and reintroduced into the injection molding machine. Any scrap that results from a thermoset manufacturing process cannot be directly recycled; most of it will end up in a landfill.

As a result of these considerations, thermoset plastics tend to lend themselves to lower production volumes due to the lower tooling cost. As production volumes increase, thermoplastics look more attractive as the savings from the lower resin costs and recyclablity start to outweigh the higher cost of the production tooling. ■

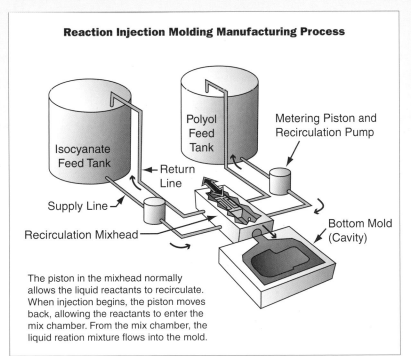

Reaction Injection Molding Manufacturing Process

Isocyanate Feed Tank

Polyol Feed Tank

Metering Piston and Recirculation Pump

Return Line

Supply Line

Recirculation Mixhead

Bottom Mold (Cavity)

The piston in the mixhead normally allows the liquid reactants to recirculate. When injection begins, the piston moves back, allowing the reactants to enter the mix chamber. From the mix chamber, the liquid reation mixture flows into the mold.

Plastic ID Chart

	Symbol & Type	Description / How to Identify	Typical Applications	Two-Part	Cyanoacrylate	Hot Melt	Methacrylate	Fusion Welding
Thermoset	PUR, RIM, RRIM Thermoset Polyurethane	Bumpers usually flexible, fenders usually rigid, usually yellow but may be gray or black, bubbles and smokes when melted.	Flexible bumper covers, fenders, dually fenders, body panels, ground effects, spoilers, snowmobile cowls	●	●	●	●	
	SMC, UP, FRP, RTM, Fiberglass	Rigid, polyester matrix reinforced with glass fibers, sands finely, dust irritating.	Street bike fairings, snowmobile cowls, rigid body panels, fenders, hoods, deck lids, header panels, spoilers, boat hulls	●	●		●	
	DCPD Dicyclopentadiene	Rigid, usually brown in color, has somewhat translucent, rough appearance on backside. (trade names Telene and Metton)	Snowmobile cowls, heavy truck hoods and cowls, agricultural equipment cowls.	●	●		●	
Thermoplastic	ABS Acrylonitrile Butadiene Styrene	Rigid, may be molded in any color (often white or black), sands finely but will melt if sanded at high speed.	Street bike fairings, instrument panels, trim moldings, consoles, armrest supports, household appliances	●	●		●	●
	EEBC Ether Ester Block Copolymer	Flexible, off-white in color, similar in appearance to PUR (trade name Lomod by GE)	Rocker cover moldings, bumper extensions (not very common)	●		●		●
	EMA Ethylene Methacrylic Acid	Semi-rigid, molded in a variety of colors, unpainted (trade name Bexloy W by DuPont)	Bumper covers (Dodge Neon 1st generation, base model. Not common)	●		●		
	PA Polyamide (Nylon)	Semi-rigid or rigid, usually black, sands finely, usually reinforced with glass, sparkles may be visible in breaks.	Radiator tanks, headlamp bezels, exterior trim parts, mirrors, intake manifolds, valve covers, other engine componentes.	●				
	PA + PPO Nylon & polyester blend	Semi-rigid, sands finely, usually off-white in color. (trade name Noryl GTX by GE Plastics)	Street bike fairings, fenders (Saturn, VW Beetle), vertical body panels (Smart Car), exterior trim.	●				
	PC + ABS Polycarbonate & ABS blend	Rigid, sands finely, usually molded in dark color (trade name Pulse by GE Plastics)	Street bike fairings, door skins (Saturn), instrument panels	●	●		●	●
	PC + PBT Polycarbonate & polyester blend	Very rigid, sands finely, usually molded in dark color (trade name Xenoy by GE Plastics)	Bumper systems and reinforcements, instrument panels, interior and exterior trim, spoilers, headlight supports.	●	●		●	●
	PE Polyethylene	Semi-flexible, melts and smears when grinding, has waxy surface feel and appearance.	ATV and dirt bike fenders and gas tanks, overflow tanks, windshield washer bottles, RV water storage tanks			●		●
	PMMA Polymethyl Methacrylic Acid	Clear or translucent material (trade names Acrylic and Lucite)	Headlight, taillight, and sidemarker lenses; street bike windshields.		●		●	
	PP Polypropylene	Semi-flexible, usually black in color, melts and smears when grinding, has waxy surface feel and appearance.	ATV fenders, bumper covers, inner fender liners, fan shrouds, gas tanks, interior trim, headlight supports	●		●		●
	PVC Polyvinyl Chloride	Rigid, usually off-white or gray in color	RV plumbing and storage tanks. Not often used in automotive or motorcycle applications.	●	●		●	●
	TPE Thermoplastic Elastomer	Flexible to semi-flexible, usually black or gray, melts and smears when grinding.	Flexible bumper covers, filler panels, fender liners. Usually closely related to TPO.	●		●		●
	TPO, TEO, PP/EPDM Thermoplastic Olefin	Semi-flexible, usually gray or black in color, melts and smears when grinding, has waxy surface feel and appearance.	Bumper covers (most common), air dams, grilles, instrument panels, headlight supports, interior & exterior trim.	●		●		●
	TPU, TPUR Thermoplastic Poilyurethane	Flexible, melts with application of heat (in contrast to the more common thermoset polyurethane)	Soft filler panels, gravel deflectors, rocker panel covers (not common)	●		●		●

rigid, it's probably Xenoy. If it's very flexible, it's probably urethane. If it's somewhere in between, it's probably TPO, but it might be urethane.

The fail-safe way to identify the plastic is to look for the identification symbol on the backside of the part. It is supposed to be molded into all plastics, but occasionally the manufacturers will miss one. Fortunately, if the ID symbol is not visible, there are other ways to identify the plastic.

Depending on what type of equipment you have available, you could do a melt test, a grinding test, or a float test to determine if you're dealing with a TPO or a PUR. The easiest way is to use an airless plastic welder and try to melt the plastic. With the welder set at the highest heat setting, lay the welder tip on the backside of the part in a concealed area. A thermoset urethane part will start to smoke and bubble immediately. A clear liquid material will also come to the surface. It will look like it's melting, but the heat is actually breaking the plastic down, causing the plasticizer to come to the surface. After this melted area cools down, touch it with your finger. If it's still sticky, you'll know you've chemically broken down the plastic, so you've got a thermoset urethane.

By contrast, if the material is a TPO, the plastic will melt cleanly and will not bubble or smoke excessively. After the melted area cools off, it will resolidify and will have the same feel as the surrounding unmelted plastic.

If you don't have an airless plastic welder available to do this test, use a high-speed, air-powered grinder with a coarse sandpaper disc and grind the backside of the part. Use the highest speed possible and apply plenty of pressure to the grinder. The friction heat from the grinder disc will generate enough heat to melt the plastic. If the material melts, smears, and gets stringy, it is a TPO. If it sands finely (like dust), it is a PUR.

Finally, you can check if the material is PUR or TPO by placing a sliver of the material into a cup of water. TPO is lighter than water and PUR is heavier. Simply cut a small sliver off a concealed edge of the plastic and run some water over it to wet it. Then push the wet sliver down into a cup of water with your finger. If it sinks, it's PUR; if it floats, it's TPO. Xenoy is also heavier than water, so if you manage to cut a sliver off the edge of a Xenoy bumper, it will sink. However, Xenoy is such a hard material, you will find it difficult to cut a sizable sliver from a bumper made of it. It's usually very easy to identify Xenoy from its rigidity alone.

Interior Plastics

Plastic interior panels have a longer history than plastic bumper fascia. Starting with armrest supports, consoles, and instrument panel trim, injection-molded thermoplastics have had a constant presence in automotive interiors since the 1960s. Prior to that, vinyl upholstery, a.k.a. Naugahyde, came into existence. Over the years, more and more components are being made from plastic, including door panels, window trim, and even entire instrument panels.

In general, plastics offer many advantages over alternate materials, such as metals, in the automotive interior. Plastics offer the ability to mold in compound curves, allowing greater styling freedom. They also provide designers with the ability to consolidate several parts into one, saving costs and easing assembly. Most impor-

Table 2.3 - Common Automotive Interior Plastics		
Plastic Type	**ID Symbols**	**ID Tips & Comments**
Vinyl & Urethane Foam	PVC, but usually no ID symbol	Commonly used on dashboard covers, door panels, and armrests. Urethane foam provides soft feel and shock absorption. Rigid pads, like on dashboards, can be repaired.
ABS	ABS	Rigid plastic. May be molded in any color. Melts and resolidifies when heated with welder.
Thermoplastic Olefin	TPO, TEO, PP+EPDM	More flexible than ABS, has slightly shiny or greasy appearance. Lighter than water. Melts and resolidifies when heated with welder.
Xenoy	PC+PBT	Very rigid. Usually molded in dark color, but may be molded in any color. Heavier than water. Melts and resolidifies when heated with welder.

tantly, they can be engineered to absorb energy, enhancing passenger safety in a collision. In fact, the introduction of plastic materials, such as padded dashboards, has probably saved hundreds, if not thousands of lives over the decades. Table 2.3 shows a few of the plastics that are most commonly used inside the car.

One of the very first applications of plastic in the automotive interior was on padded dashboards. These pads were constructed of a thermoset urethane foam pad covered with a vinyl (PVC, or polyvinyl chloride) skin that helped absorb collision impact. Urethane foam is the most common thermoset plastic used in automotive interiors; most others are thermoplastic.

The most common interior plastic is ABS (acrylonitrile butadiene styrene). ABS is a versatile, easily moldable, and inexpensive resin that is used to create instrument panel trim, consoles, armrest supports, door panels, and so on. ABS is easy to paint and it can also be molded in a variety of colors. These features are important because interior parts are very appearance-critical, especially dashboard components.

As on bumper fascia, polypropylene and TPO are making major inroads into the vehicle interior due to their low cost. Much development has been done with TPOs to provide the same surface quality and soft feel of vinyl-covered urethane foam at a much lower cost. In the early 2000s, North America saw its first domestically produced all-TPO dashboard with the Ford Focus, and TPOs are expected to take a major market share from the more traditional plastics as time goes on. TPOs are also being used on door panels, column trim, and center consoles.

Polycarbonate blends, like Xenoy, are also used in the interior, but more sparingly as a result of their higher cost. Because of its high strength, polycarbonate is ideal for complex dashboard support structures. Combining several steel stampings with a single molded polycarbonate part saves cost due to parts consolidation and improves quality by eliminating several possible sources of error in the manufacturing process. Look for polycarbonate blends on load-bearing components in the car's interior.

Underhood Plastics

Plastics began making headway under the hood in the 1970s and are now used in practically every area other than the block and head (and one company has experimented with that, by the way!) Plastic was initially used on parts like overflow bottles and windshield washer bottles, and later expanded to air cleaner boxes and ducts. Radiator tanks made the switch to plastic in the 1980s, replacing brass. Now oil pans, valve covers, and intake manifolds are being made with plastic.

The four most common types of plastic under the hood are polyethylene, polypropylene, nylon, and thermoplastic polyester. Table 2.4 shows a few of the plastics that are most commonly used inside the car. Polyethylene is usually molded in a "natural" color, which is a translucent white. This is the material used to make overflow and washer bottles. It is also used for battery cases and fluid reservoirs. Because it is so inert and resistant to chemical attack, polyethylene is the material of choice whenever any fluid has to be contained.

Table 2.4 - Common Automotive Underhood Plastics		
Plastic Type	**ID Symbols**	**ID Tips & Comments**
Polyethylene	PE, LDPE, HDPE	Usually molded in translucent white or "natural" color. Semi-rigid. Has an oily feel. Melts easily with airless welder; melted area resolidifies. Sliver floats in water.
Polypropylene or TPO	PP, TPO, PP + EPDM, TEO	Usually molded in black. Semi rigid. Has an oily feel. Melts easily with airless welder; melted area resolidifies. Sliver floats in water.
Nylon (Polyamide)	PA, PA-6, PA-66	Usually molded in black or dark brown. Very rigid. Slick surface, but not an oily feel. Not easily melted; has high melting point. Melted area resolidifies. Melted area may appear to have sparkles (which are the glass fibers).
Polyester (Thermoplastic)	PET, PBT	Usually molded in black. Very rigid. Shiny surface, but not an oily feel. Melts easier than nylon with airless welder. Melted area resolidifies. Melted area may appear to have sparkles (which are the glass fibers).

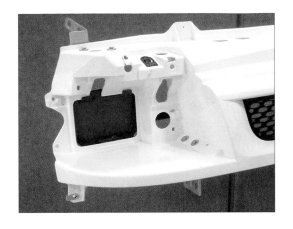

Components with highly complex shapes can be made economically with sheet-molding compounds (SMC). Here we see a header panel before and after installation on a vehicle. (courtesy of SMC Alliance)

Polypropylene is closely related to polyethylene as it is an *olefin* plastic. It is also quite resistant to chemical attack. It may also be used to contain fluids, but it is more often used on filler panels, undertrays, fan shrouds, and engine covers. It is usually molded in black and has a slick or greasy appearance and feel.

Nylon, having one of the highest softening point temperatures of all plastics, is preferred when the plastic must be in contact with hot surfaces or fluids. Good examples are radiator tanks and oil pans. The nylon used in high temperature applications is usually reinforced with glass fibers for additional strength.

Like nylon, thermoplastic polyester (PET or PBT) is usually reinforced with glass fibers. Its heat resistance is also quite high, but polyester is usually used for structural components such as grille supports, radiator supports, or headlight supports.

Automotive Body Panels

Despite the fact that even today most automotive body panels are still made of steel, the very first applications of plastic in the industry were actually for body panels. Popularly known as *fiberglass,* glass-reinforced thermoset polyester composites or FRP (fiber reinforced plastics) were actually developed back in the 1940s, mainly for the aerospace industry. One of the first volume-produced, FRP-bodied cars was the 1953 Chevrolet Corvette.

Composite body panels moved from labor-intensive fiberglass to a more production-oriented sheet-molding compound (SMC) in the 1970s. The number of SMC applications has exploded since then, being used on header panels, pickup truck boxes, hoods, deck lids, tailgates, fenders, and in the case of the first-generation GM minivans, even entire bodies.

General Motors has been the leader in plastic body panel production. Of course, the Corvette has always had a composite body, but because it has a fairly low production volume, it's always made good economic sense to produce it in plastic. GM's first high-volume car with plastic outer body panels was the 1984 Pontiac Fiero. The Fiero actually used a variety of plastic materials including nylon, thermoset polyurethane, and SMC. These panels were hung on an underlying steel unibody. Part of GM's reasoning for using plastic was that it enabled them to make styling changes more often without changing the basic structure of the vehicle. GM did make one major styling revision to the car before its commercial demise in 1988.

GM used the same structural design on their first-generation minivans, except all the panels were SMC. Unfortunately, these vans were not a big commercial success partly due to the vans' unusual styling. GM's most successful car with plastic body panels has been its line of Saturn vehicles. In fact, the plastic body panels are so popular that they have become an integral part of the Saturn identity.

At the time of this writing, the continued advance of plastic body panels shows no sign of slowing. OEMs will continue to press forward with plastics for greater cost savings and styling freedom. Some of the research being done now shows the direction body panel plastics will go. The trend toward less expensive resins, such as

Modern street bikes, such as this Suzuki Hayabusa, are built with many plastic components, typically ABS or ABS derivatives. (courtesy of Suzuki Motor Corp.)

TPO, will continue. Improvements are continuously being made to TPOs to enable them to be used in more demanding applications like fenders and door skins. In Europe, Ford's Th!nk car has debuted with rotationally molded, molded-in-color, polyethylene body panels.

The paint process has always been a problem for the OEMs because of its volatile organic compound (VOC) emissions. Also, many of the plastics can't stand up to the temperatures of the bake ovens used to cure paint on metal, so plastic parts often have to be painted off-line using a separate process. OEMs are developing new processes to eliminate the paint step altogether. Standard TPO plastics are being covered with a paintlike film so that when they pop out of the mold, they already look painted. Also, advances are being made in creating plastics that are molded in color, some with a metallic appearance. Over the next decade or two, we will undoubtedly see a car that rolls from the assembly line with no paint used on the outer body panels at all.

Because of the environmental benefits and potentially large cost savings of eliminating the paint step, body panel plastics will be the most active area of development in the near future.

Motorcycle Plastics

Although it's difficult to believe today, prior to the 1970s, virtually every part of a motorcycle was crafted from metal. In the old days, even off-road motorcycles sported aluminum gas tanks and fenders. Today, both dirt and street bikes utilize plastic components and body panels to the point where, at least on street bikes, little metal is visible on the machine.

Motorcycle production volumes are generally lower than those of automobiles, so it makes economic sense to create components from plastic rather than metal to reduce the tooling costs. Although by no means cheap, injection molding tooling is less expensive than stamps and forms for making sheet metal parts. Plastic also allows for greater styling flexibility and lower weight, both of which are very important for motorcycle applications.

The plastics used on on-road and off-road motorcycles were basically separated at birth. Dirt bikes and ATVs have always utilized molded-in-color, low-density polyethylene parts because of their toughness and chemical resistance. Street bikes have tended to use non-olefin engineering thermoplastics like ABS, PC, and nylon for their body panels. Because of this clear separation, I will discuss the plastics used on dirt and street bikes separately.

Street Bikes

Street bike parts are good candidates for repair for three reasons. First, they tend to be very expensive. They are also easy to repair using a variety of methods. Finally, fillers and paints stick to these plastics well, making it easy to end up with a part that looks as good as new.

The fairings, sidecovers, tailpieces, and tank covers of most modern, mass-produced street bikes are made of one of three types of plastic: ABS, an ABS/PC blend, or a nylon blend. Straight ABS is the most common, as it is the least expensive resin of the group. Polycarbonate can be blended into ABS to increase its strength, allowing for thinner, lighter panels, but it is also makes the resin more expensive. For this reason, PC blends are somewhat rare. Reinforced nylon blends, like the GTX from GE Plastics, are more flexible and tougher than ABS, but they also are more expensive.

Fortunately for the technician, most street bike parts are well marked with ID symbols on

The SMC Manufacturing Process

Sheet molding compound is unique among thermoset manufacturing techniques in that it uses a two-step process. The sheet form of the product is first made and rolled up for later processing. This roll is usually transported to the final processor's facility, where it is unrolled, trimmed, and pressed into final shape.

SMC consists of about 25 percent by weight of long glass fibers (1/2 to two inches long), a high viscosity thermoset polyester resin, and mineral fillers. The polyester resin/filler paste is first deposited onto a moving polyethylene carrier film. The glass fibers are then deposited on top of the resin in a random pattern. Finally, another layer of resin paste is deposited on top of the glass fibers. Another layer of polyethylene film goes on top of that, then the sandwich is compacted to ensure good penetration of resin into the glass fiber strands. This "green" SMC is then wound up into rolls, ready for final processing.

At the final processing stage, the SMC sheet is unrolled and trimmed to size. The polyethylene carrier

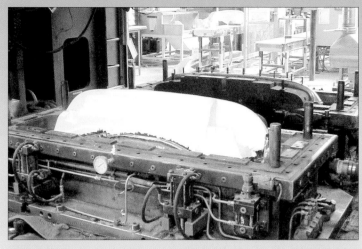

Note the depth and complexity of this SMC part. SMC molding allows deeper draws and more surface detail than steel stamping.

films are stripped off and the SMC blank is placed in a mold. The mold is closed, compressed, and heated to about 300 degrees F. The heat catalyzes the polyester resin, causing it to harden in the mold. Cure time can range from one to five minutes, depending on the size of the part.

The compressive forces in an SMC press are quite high (between 250 to 2000 psi), so sturdy steel molds must be created and large, expensive presses must be used. Despite this, the cost of an SMC press can be only one-fifth that of a corresponding metal stamping press. As a result, SMC is an excellent material choice for low to medium-low production volumes. Because the material cost of SMC is higher than that of steel, as production volumes increase, the savings in the material cost of steel start to outweigh the initial tooling investment. ∎

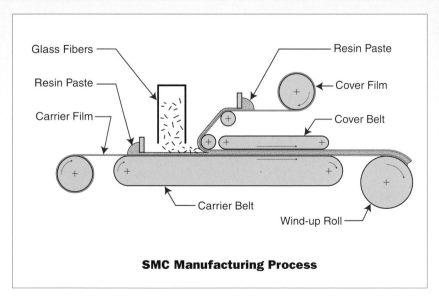

SMC Manufacturing Process

the backside. Table 2.5 shows the ID symbol for each type of plastic used on street bikes and some tips for identifying the plastic if you can't find the symbol. Once you've determined the plastic used, skip to Chapter 3 of this book for tips on deciding the best repair method.

Aftermarket motorcycle body parts, such as fairings, sidecovers, or saddlebags, are generally made from FRP, a.k.a. fiberglass. This is the material of choice for low-production volumes because the tooling is so inexpensive. You can usually tell this material by the rough surface on the backside of the part. You'll be able to see a woven cloth pattern or a random pattern of fibers. When fiberglass breaks, it's very easy to identify because of the fine glass fibers that will jut out into the broken area.

A few mass-produced saddlebags and fairings are made from SMC. This material is similar to FRP, except that it is smooth on both sides of the part. If it breaks, you'll see a multitude of glass fibers in the cracked area

Dirt Bikes and ATVs

Plastics for dirt bikes and ATVs are not the best candidates for repair for three reasons. First, they are usually not as outrageously expensive as street bike parts, making it more likely that you will choose to replace the part. Second, they can only be repaired using a plastic welder. Finally, they will not accept fillers or paint at all, so you can't get them looking perfect again.

Dirt bike and ATV fenders are almost always made from low-density polyethylene, but sometimes you may see them made of polypropylene. Both of these plastics are olefin materials, meaning that they're naturally oily. Olefin plastics have a low surface energy, making them quite inert to chemical attack. That's why this material is often used on fuel tanks.

Because of their naturally oily feel, polyolefins are ideal for dirt bikes because mud and dirt don't stick well, allowing the mud-encrusted dirt machine to be washed more easily. Conversely, it makes them difficult to repair because it keeps adhesives and paint from sticking well to them as well.

On most plastics, after completing a plastic repair by welding or adhesive, the cosmetic surface is sanded smooth and painted. However, because adhesives, fillers, and paint don't stick to polyethylene, you can't make a perfect repair on this type of plastic. Only weld repairs can be done, so you'll have to live with its welded appearance.

In addition, all dirt bike plastics are molded in color and usually have a somewhat transparent appearance, so even if you could paint the part, it wouldn't look original anyway.

But you can make a repair that will restore the part's function and get you back on the trail again. Polyethylene and polypropylene are both easily welded using either airless or hot-air welding techniques. Furthermore, these easily meltable plastics may be reinforced by melting a stainless steel wire screen into the plastic. The mesh strengthens the repair by transferring stresses into the undamaged base material. See how to perform such repairs in Chapter 4.

Recreational Vehicles

Sales of recreational vehicles, such as snowmobiles, personal watercraft, and RVs have risen dramatically since the early '90s. Most of these machines sport a variety of plastic body panels and parts. In this section, I'll briefly cover the general types of plastic used on these types of

Table 2.5 - Plastics Commonly Used on Street Bikes		
Type of Plastic	Description/How to Identify	Typical Usage
ABS (Acrylonitrile Butadiene Styrene)	Rigid; sands finely. Color does not give reliable indication.	Fairings, side panels, tailpieces.
PC + ABS (Polycarbonate and ABS Blend)	Rigid; sands finely. Similar to pure ABS except stronger and more rigid. Color does not give reliable indication, but typically molded in dark colors.	Fairings, side panels, tailpieces.
PA (Polyamide, a.k.a. Nylon), PA+PPE Blends	Semi-rigid; more flexible than ABS or PC+ABS. Usually molded in lighter colors.	Fairings, side panels, tailpieces.
SMC, UP, FRP	Rigid; polyester matrix reinforced with glass fibers, usually thicker than injection molded plastics; sands finely.	Fairings; more common on aftermarket products.

equipment. These markets are more fragmented, so the types of plastic used are not as standardized as they are with cars and motorcycles. If you run into a plastic that's not described here, refer to the Plastic ID chart on earlier in this chapter.

Snowmobiles

Many people in the northern United States and Canada make the best of the winter season by having some fun on their snowmobiles. As with any other sport in which fragile machines are ridden at high speed through treacherous terrain, crashes happen. And when crashes happen, parts break.

One of the most commonly damaged parts on a snowmobile is its cowl, the large plastic part that covers the engine. When the snowmobile flips or rolls, the cowl can suffer a lot of damage.

Replacement cowls for snowmobiles can cost upwards of $500, so the incentive to repair these parts is obvious. The four major manufacturers, Arctic Cat, Polaris, Ski-Doo, and Yamaha, all tend to use different materials, but the general trend for all of the manufacturers is a move toward TPO.

Most Arctic Cat cowls are typically made from a rigid thermoset plastic material that is popularly known as either Metton or Telene (Metton is made by Metton America, Telene by B.F. Goodrich). These are reaction injection molding (RIM) materials that are similar to polyurethanes in their manufacture except that they are based on dicyclopentadiene (DCPD) chemistry. Being a thermoset material, DCPD will not melt with the application of heat. It, therefore, must be repaired using an adhesive. These types of plastic are usually dark brown on the backside, and their appearance is somewhat translucent and non-homogeneous.

The manufacturers of both Metton and Telene recommend the use of two-part adhesives for repair. There are two-part epoxy and urethane adhesives available from a wide range of manufacturers that will work well for repairing Metton. To learn how to repair rigid plastics using two-part adhesives see Chapter 4.

Up until 1998, Polaris also used DCPD thermoset material in its cowls. Polaris is now

Polyolefins are commonly used on recreational vehicles, such as this ATV, because their "oily" surfaces resist holding mud and grime and make them easy to clean. (courtesy of Suzuki Motor Corp.)

making the transition to TPO for the same reason the auto manufacturers are: it's cheaper.

The TPO cowls can be identified because they are more flexible than the older DCPD units. TPO will melt immediately upon being touched with the hot welder tip. It will also melt and smear when ground with sandpaper at high speed. TPO may be repaired by a variety of methods, including two-part adhesive, fusion welding, or hot-melt adhesive.

In the majority of Ski-Doo sleds, a very flexible thermoset polyurethane (PUR) is used to make the cowls. This is the most durable material used by any of the manufacturers, able to withstand severe abuse. They can break, however. PUR may be repaired with either two-part adhesives or with the airless plastic welder. Both of these repair techniques can create a strong, durable, and flexible repair.

Ski-Doo also uses TPO, and I predict that they will convert more applications to TPO in the future. Ski-Doo's PUR cowls are yellowish-white in color while the TPO units are black, so they're easy to tell apart.

Through 1996, Yamaha used SMC in its cowls almost exclusively. This material is very rigid and can be easily identified by the glass fibers that become visible when it cracks. SMC is easily repaired using rigid two-part epoxy or urethane adhesives.

In 1997, Yamaha began switching its cowls to a TPO blend that is off-white in color and has the ID symbol "PP+T20" molded into the backside. As you can see, every manufacturer is transitioning to TPO, so chances are, if you have a late-model sled, you'll be dealing with a TPO.

Personal Watercraft

For decades, boat hulls have been made using hand-laid fiber-reinforced plastic (FRP), popularly known as fiberglass. Anyone who has worked with fiberglass before can testify that it's a stinky, nasty, itchy business. The styrene fumes emanating from the polyester resin can cause environmental and health problems, and all those invisibly small glass fibers seem to get embedded in every pore of your skin, causing you to itch for days. Manufacturers have long sought to move away from this material, but due to the large size of most boat hulls and the relatively small production volumes they require, there just hasn't been a better way to make them.

Personal watercraft, like Jet-Skis, are another story. They have a lower price point, allowing their production volumes to be higher, and they also are physically smaller in size than traditional boat hulls. Because of these two factors, manufacturers have been able to justify investing in the relatively expensive production tooling required to make the hulls from sheet-molding composite (SMC). SMC is much more amenable to mass production. It is a much cleaner and more consistent manufacturing process than is hand-laid FRP.

SMC can be identified by the multitude of glass fibers that are visible in the damaged area. SMC is easily repaired using rigid two-part epoxy or urethane adhesives.

Some personal watercraft hulls are also manufactured using thermoformed acrylic sheets.

Because acrylic sheet is similar in thickness and rigidity to SMC, it is difficult to tell them apart unless they are broken, but the acrylic material will not have the glass fiber reinforcement that SMC has. There are two other ways to distinguish acrylics from SMC: 1) Acrylics will be glossy on the backside, whereas SMC will usually be flat gray or off-white, and 2) Acrylics will be the same color on the backside and the frontside, whereas SMC is always painted. The repair technique, however, would be the same as for SMC two-part rigid adhesive.

Travel Coaches and Trailers

In my seven years serving as technical support manager for Urethane Supply Company, a plastic repair product manufacturer, I have received dozens, if not hundreds, of questions from RV owners and repair technicians. Every single question, without exception, referred to the repair of the water storage tanks. I know there are plenty of other plastic parts on RVs, but it seems like the holding tank is the only thing that gives anyone problems.

The holding tanks on an RV, like practically any other plastic used to contain liquids, are made from either polyethylene or polypropylene. Between these two, polyethylene is the material of choice in the vast majority of cases. Polyolefins, like PE and PP, are the materials of choice because of their chemical inertness and low manufacturing cost.

Due to their inherent oiliness, polyolefins are difficult to repair with adhesives, so welding is the best repair option for these plastics. Fusion welding is also the preferred option for repairing fluid storage tanks, as the repair will resist chemical attack just as well as the base material. If adhesives are used in such conditions, especially on PE and PP, the fluid may attack the adhesive itself or find a way between the adhesive and base material.

Some of the plumbing on RVs may be PVC or ABS. Both of these plastics are easily fusion welded. For pipe fittings, the easiest method is solvent welding.

Repair Options for Each Type of Plastic

Once you have identified the plastic you're working with, it's time to repair it. The next problem will be figuring out which repair method to use for the type of plastic you've got.

In this chapter, I'll briefly introduce the different repair methods here to familiarize you with them, and then I'll explore each different type of plastic and discuss the preferred repair options for each. At the end of this section, I'll summarize the pros and cons of each repair method for each type of plastic in an easy-to-reference table.

Repair Technologies

There are several different products and methods available for repairing plastics. A particular method might work very well on one type of plastic and not at all on another. That's why I strongly recommend identifying the plastic before deciding on the repair method. Now that you've identified the plastic, it's time to decide on the best repair method.

There are five generic types of plastic repair technologies covered in this book. All repair technologies fall under two main categories—adhesives or welding—described in Table 3.1.

Adhesives are the most commonly used repair process and may be used on virtually every type of plastic. However, there are a few types of plastic that are so slippery that adhesives just won't work. In these cases, plastic welding is the only way to go. Chapter 4 details how to make repairs using either method.

| Table 3.1 - Repair Technologies ||
Adhesives	Welding
Two-Part Adhesives Cyanoacrylate (CA) Adhesives Hot-Melt Adhesives Methacrylate Adhesives	Fusion Welding

There is also another welding method—solvent welding—that I will not cover in this book. Certain types of plastic (PVC and ABS, in particular) can be softened with the appropriate solvent and joined while softened. This is the most common way of joining PVC pipe, but it is not used in doing plastic repair work of the type covered in this book.

Thermoset Plastics

Thermoset plastics are solid plastic materials that have been created via a chemical reaction between two components. Once the chemical reaction is complete, the plastic can neither be melted (it can be destroyed by heat, but it cannot be softened and reformed like a thermoplastic), nor can it be broken back down into its constituent components again. The creation of a thermoset part is a one-way process. By contrast, thermoplastics can be softened and reformed with heat.

Thermosets are very common on vehicular applications and, thankfully, they are generally very easy to repair. The main distinction between thermosets and thermoplastics with regard to repair procedures is that thermosets, naturally, cannot be fusion welded, as they are not themselves meltable. Therefore, adhesives are the only way to repair thermosets. Two-part adhesives are by far the most common method of repair for thermosets. Cyanoacrylate and methacrylate adhesives also work well on rigid thermosets. Surprisingly, an airless plastic welder may also be used to apply a hot-melt adhesive onto flexible thermosets.

In this section, I'll discuss each of the thermoset plastic materials commonly found on automobiles, motorcycles, and recreational vehicles and the best methods of repair for each.

Fiberglass

Fiberglass is the common term for FRP (fiber reinforced plastic). This is a composite structure consisting of a fiber reinforcement embedded in a thermoset polyester or epoxy resin. Because they are inexpensive, glass fibers are by far the most common type of fiber used to reinforce such structures, hence the name fiberglass. However, structures using Kevlar or carbon fiber reinforcement are also used when demand for strength and stiffness outweigh the cost considerations. Carbon-fiber-reinforced composites have recently become very common in demanding applications such as race car chassis structures.

Fiberglass also refers to the manufacturing process by which the material is made, as distinguished from its close relative, SMC. Fiberglass structures are created using largely a manual process. The usual process is that a *gel coat* is first applied inside a female mold. The gel coat creates the smooth finish on the outer surface of the finished part. Gel coat is basically a polyester-resin based paint that provides both the cosmetic outer surface and the outer layer of resin into which the fiber reinforcement will embed itself. After the gel coat is sprayed in, the fiberglass or other fiber reinforcement is laid on top of the gel coat. On smaller components, a sheet of fiberglass cloth is typically laid in by hand. On larger products, such as boat hulls, the fiber might be sprayed on using a chopper gun. After the fiber is laid into the mold, polyester or epoxy resin is brushed or sprayed onto the backside of the cloth.

The strength of the composite structure depends on completely encasing the glass fibers with resin. During the manufacturing process, great care is taken to ensure that all the glass fibers are wetted with the resin. When using a clear resin, this is easy to determine because the glass fiber mat will turn from a white color to transparent when it is completely wetted. A tool called a *saturation roller* is used to work the resin into the glass mat.

It is also important to the strength of the structure to remove all the air bubbles that may form within the laminate. In critical applications such as race car chassis or aircraft parts, air bubbles are forced out by pressure using a vacuum bagging process. This additional step is usually not required for the types of parts you'll usually find on cars and motorcycles.

With the exception of early Corvettes, there are not any fiberglass parts produced for cars or motorcycles at the OEM level. The manufacturing process is simply too labor intensive to make it economical at larger production levels. The OEMs use a lot of SMC, which is the mass-production cousin of fiberglass. I'll explore SMC in the next section. If you do find a fiberglass part on a car or motorcycle, it is almost certain to be a component produced by an aftermarket company. On cars you might find aftermarket restyling kits such as ground effects, spoilers, diffusers, and wings made from fiberglass, as well as fairings and aftermarket body kits.

Fiberglass is easy to identify because it is rough on the backside and smooth on the front. You will be able to see the texture of the glass cloth on the backside, whether it is woven or random fibers. Also if it is cracked or damaged, you'll be able to see the raw glass fiber cloth exposed, especially if the part is made from a woven bi-directional cloth.

Fiberglass is extremely easy to repair using a variety of adhesives. The most popular adhesive is fiberglass resin, available in any hardware store. This is usually a clear, liquid, polyester resin, probably of exactly the same type that was used to manufacture the part in the first place. Fiberglass resin has a relatively low viscosity to enable it to soak into the fiber mat—a requirement for the manufacturing process. However, low viscosity adhesives are difficult to use when making repairs, particularly on vertical surfaces, as the resin tends to run downhill before it sets up.

When doing repairs on fiberglass, it is easier and faster to use a two-part epoxy or urethane-based repair compound. These have a high viscosity, allowing them to remain in place, even on a vertical surface, while the thermosetting chemical reaction is taking place. Adhesion of these repair materials on fiberglass is outstanding. If the repair is reinforced with additional fiberglass cloth and sufficient backing material is used, the repair area can actually be made stronger than the original part.

Cyanoacrylates also stick well to fiberglass and are excellent for tacking broken parts back together. However, for the ultimate in durability, I would recommend completing the repair with a two-part material. Methacrylate adhesives stick well to fiberglass and would be well suited for replacing missing details or filling holes.

The only adhesive that wouldn't work on fiberglass would be a hot-melt. Although a hot-melt might stick adequately to the surface, it wouldn't be suited for a structural repair as hot-melts tend to be flexible by nature.

Table 3.2 gives some general rules of thumb for the types of damage each repair method is best suited for.

SMC

Since the 1980s, car manufacturers, particularly those in North America, have made increasing use of SMC (sheet molding composite) as a replacement for steel body panels. SMC is common for tailgates, hoods, fenders, doors, and pickup truck boxes. All of the body panels on GM's first-generation minivans were made of SMC, as are the body panels on the Corvette, Dodge Viper, and Chrysler Prowler.

SMC has a couple of advantages over sheet-metal. First of all, SMC is a bit lighter than a comparable steel component and has a bit more styling flexibility due to its ability to form sharp bends and compound curves. Also, the tooling

Table 3.2 - Repair Methods for Fiberglass Parts	
Repair Method	**Comments**
Two-Part Adhesives	Polyester or epoxy resin is the best choice for manufacturing fiberglass parts and for doing many repairs. Epoxy or urethane two-part repair materials are often faster and easier to use for most repair work.
Cyanoacrylate (CA)	Great for tacking broken parts back together. Will not withstand continual stress or vibration unless reinforced with epoxy or urethane two-part material.
Hot-Melt	Not recommended, as most hot-melt adhesives are flexible.
Methacrylate	Good for repairing details or small holes.
Plastic Fusion Welding	Fiberglass cannot be fusion welded.

and machinery used to create SMC parts are less expensive than those used to make sheet-metal parts, so it makes sense to use SMC on vehicles where the production volumes are likely to be on the low side, such as on the Chrysler Prowler.

The disadvantages of SMC include a higher part cost than steel and the difficulty of recycling. Regardless, SMC's popularity is likely to grow as OEMs become more and more familiar with the material and become more clever as to how to engineer parts to take advantage of SMC's strengths.

SMC creates a composite structure similar to that of fiberglass, that is, both consist of glass fibers within a thermoset resin matrix. SMC's chemistry differs from fiberglass in that its resin system is heat-cured, which enables its unique manufacturing process (see sidebar for full details on how SMC is produced). Basically, SMC is created in sheet form and rolled up on coils, similar to coils of sheet metal. At this stage the SMC resin is soft enough to allow it to be rolled into coils. These coils are shipped to the factory where they will be molded into their final shape. This two-stage manufacturing process is unique among thermosets.

The "green" SMC is unrolled, trimmed, and pressed in a tool that forms it into its final shape

Table 3.3 - Repair Methods for SMC Parts

Repair Method	Comments
Two-Part Adhesives	Rigid epoxy or urethane two-part repair materials are the best method for repair. Do not use fiberglass resins as they are not compatible with SMC. Best results are obtained by first using a CA to bond the broken pieces together, then using a rigid two-part to complete the repair.
Cyanoacrylate (CA)	Great for bonding broken parts back together. Will act as a structural repair if there is sufficient overlapping surface area.
Hot-Melt	Not recommended, as most hot-melt adhesives are flexible.
Methacrylate	Excellent for restoring missing tabs, flanges, and stripped threads.
Plastic Fusion Welding	SMC cannot be fusion welded.

while heating it. The part is held in this position for a few minutes until the heat has caused the resin to catalyze and harden. The part is then pulled from the mold and the rough edges are trimmed off.

Like fiberglass, SMC is a very rigid plastic. The whole part may flex over a very large radius, but a small section of the part will not flex over a small radius. Unlike fiberglass, SMC is smooth on both sides, so it is easy to distinguish from fiberglass. Furthermore, if SMC is cracked or damaged, it can also be identified by the riot of glass fibers protruding from the damaged area.

Due to its rigidity and high surface energy, SMC is easy to repair with two-part adhesives. A word of caution: do *not* use a standard polyester fiberglass resin to repair SMC. The resins are not compatible; at the very least, the repair area will become visible underneath the paint, and may debond in the worst case. The best way to repair SMC is with a rigid two-part epoxy or urethane repair material.

Cyanoacrylate adhesives (CA) work very well in repairing cracks in SMC and many times may make a perfectly adequate structural repair in themselves. If all the broken glass fibers in the cracked area can be fitted together tightly, an enormous surface area is created over which the CA can embed itself, resulting in outstanding strength. Even if you plan to reinforce the repair with a two-part adhesive, I recommend using a CA to bond the broken pieces back together first. Two-part materials are too viscous to get down into all the fibers in the cracked area, so the repair won't be as strong as it would be if you used the epoxy in combination with a CA.

Methacrylate adhesives also bond very well to SMC and are excellent for replacing missing tabs or flanges. Methacrylates can also be used to repair stripped threads in SMC. This is especially useful as many radiator and grille supports are made from SMC panels. Many of the adjoining components thread directly into the SMC. Methacrylate adhesives are unique in their ability to restore stripped threads

Table 3.3 gives some general rules of thumb for the types of damage each repair method is best suited for.

Polyurethane

Polyurethane, commonly called *urethane* for short, is unique among the thermoset plastics in that it is the only one that is flexible. Depending on the formulation, urethane can range from soft to rigid, but it is most commonly used on vehicular applications in a flexible formulation.

By far the most common application of polyurethane is for flexible bumper fascia. Back in the early 1970s, when the automotive safety movement really got its start, polyurethane was the first material used to cover the energy-absorbing structure. Urethane is easily moldable into compound curves and sharp corners, so it provides designers with a lot of freedom to style as they wish. The 1973 Corvette, first with urethane bumper fascia, could not have complied with the new energy absorbing regulations of that year and retained its sleek appearance without the use of flexible urethane covers.

Although it has largely been supplanted by TPO as the material of choice for bumper fascia, polyurethane is still popular and continues to be used in about 20 percent of late-model vehicles. Polyurethane tends to be used more often on luxury cars or other cars with lower production volumes for a couple of reasons. First, urethane provides a better painted surface finish, despite major improvements by TPO in recent years. Second and most importantly, due to their lower injection pressures, the tooling cost for creating urethane parts is less than that for creating thermoplastic parts, making it easier to break even on the cost of the tool.

Polyurethane may also be used on fenders, spoilers, air dams, lower body cladding, pickup truck boxes, and dually fenders. The latter two applications would use a more rigid polyurethane formulation and would likely be reinforced with glass. This process is known as RRIM, or reinforced reaction injection molding.

Urethane is not commonly used on motorcycle applications, but it is fairly common on snowmobile cowls, especially those of Ski-Doo. Urethane is a popular engineering material due fact that it can be molded in varying degrees of flexibility, its tooling costs are comparatively low, it accepts paint well, and it is tough and impact resistant.

Urethane's natural color is clear or yellow, but may be molded in virtually any color. Some late-model bumper covers are gray, which may cause some confusion with TPO during the identification process. The best way to tell gray urethane apart from TPO is to try to melt the bumper on the backside with a hot welder tip. If thermoset urethane is touched with a hot iron, the material will smoke and bubble immediately, whereas TPO will melt cleanly.

Due to their relatively high surface energy, urethane is easy to repair with a variety of adhesives. Its flexibility, however, presents a challenge for repair and refinish materials alike. Fortunately, there are a wide variety of adhesives available for the repair of urethane on the market. Two-parts are the most popular type of adhesive for the repair of urethane. Hot-melts are also very common and have their own advantages over two-parts. Finally, cyanoacrylates and methacrylates will stick to rigid urethane, but will not be compatible with flexible substrates. Obviously, fusion welding is out of the question as most urethanes are thermoset, or non-meltable plastics.

Table 3.4 gives some general rules of thumb for the types of damage for which each repair method is best suited.

To summarize, a two-part repair material will be your best choice for repairing a thermoset polyurethane part unless you already have a plastic welder, in which case you might also elect to repair using a hot-melt technique. If you find yourself doing lots of urethane repairs, it will be more economical to repair using hot-melts as the material costs are lower than they are for two-parts. Cyanoacrylates are effective for holding cracks together while you perform a two-part or hot-melt repair.

Other Thermoset Plastics

There may be other thermoset plastics based on a variety of chemistries other than those we've already discussed. However, there is only one that is used in any volume and worthy of discussion and that is dicyclopentadiene, or DCPD. Two popular trade names for this material are Metton and Telene. I'll refer to both as "Metton" as this is the more common of the two.

Table 3.4 - Repair Methods for Thermoset Polyurethane Parts	
Repair Method	**Comments**
Two-Part Adhesives	Most popular and easiest repair method. Flexible and rigid formulations are available to match the durometer of the substrate. Adhesive may be of urethane, epoxy, or acrylic composition.
Cyanoacrylate (CA)	Great for tacking broken pieces or cracks back together. Will break if part is flexed, so flexible repairs need to be done with two-part or hot-melt adhesive.
Hot-Melt	Fast and economical way to repair flexible urethanes. Some hot-melts do not feather well and will need to be skim coated with a flexible epoxy two-part for cosmetic finishing.
Methacrylate	Sticks well to urethane, but will break if part is flexed. Not recommended on flexible substrates.
Plastic Fusion Welding	PUR cannot be fusion welded.

As I discussed in the previous section, Metton is used as a snowmobile cowl material, particularly on Arctic Cat sleds. Its use has largely given way to TPO, but it may still be found on older machines. Metton is also used for heavy truck cowls and on agricultural equipment.

It may be difficult to determine if a part is Metton or some other rigid thermoplastic. It is not so important to make a clear determination of the exact composition of the material. If the part is rigid and you know that it is thermoset, then the best repair method is a two-part repair material. You may consider the part as being made of SMC and follow the same procedure for repairing it. Table 3.5 provides rules of thumb for repairing Metton and other unidentifiable rigid thermoset materials.

Thermoplastics

Thermoplastics are the most common *plastic* material. They are characterized by the fact that they may be melted and resolidified. Due to this fact, thermoplastics may usually be repaired using plastic welding techniques in addition to adhesive techniques. Some thermoplastics, particularly rigid plastics, may be better suited for adhesive repairs. In this section, I'll consider each family of thermoplastic material and discuss the pros and cons of each repair method.

Polypropylene and TPO

TPO (a.k.a TEO) is a blend of a polyolefin, usually polypropylene (PP) and an elastomer (usually a synthetic rubber, like EPDM), usually with PP forming the continuous phase and the rubber being added to improve flexibility and impact resistance. TPOs are blended with other plastics and chemicals to modify a whole range of different physical properties.

There are dozens of different companies producing TPO materials. Due to their high engineering properties-to-cost ratio, there is more research and development work being done on TPOs than any other type of plastic. As a result, no two TPOs on the market are exactly the same. There are thousands of different blends of TPO on the market formulated for everything from wire insulation to car bumpers.

Table 3.5 - Repair Methods for Rigid Thermoset Plastics	
Repair Method	**Comments**
Two-Part Adhesives	Rigid epoxy or urethane two-part repair materials are the only option for durable repairs.
Cyanoacrylate (CA)	May work for tacking broken parts back together.
Hot-Melt	Not recommended, as most hot-melt adhesives are flexible.
Methacrylate	May be used for restoring missing tabs, flanges, bosses, and stripped threads. Test adhesion first using a test bond.
Plastic Fusion Welding	Rigid thermosets cannot be fusion welded.

Because of the diversity of formulations in TPO, fusion welding repair techniques are difficult to perform because of incompatibility between the welding rod and the base material. Fusion welding could easily be performed *if* you had a close match between the welding rod and substrate. Sometimes you get lucky. Bumpers on Honda automobiles have a low elastomer content and are thus easy to weld using a polypropylene welding rod. However, because the elastomer percentage in TPOs can range from zero to over 50 percent, it's hard to find a single fusion welding rod that can repair all TPOs.

Because it is a polyolefin (or "oily" plastic), many adhesives also have a hard time with TPO. Polyolefins have low surface energy, which means that any adhesive or coating applied to it would rather stick to itself than "wet out" on the surface of the plastic. It's hard to get good adhesion when your adhesive doesn't get into all the microscopic nooks and crannies in the plastic's surface.

Adhesion can be improved by applying an *adhesion promoter* or *surface modifier* prior to application of the adhesive. All repair product manufacturers have systems that work on TPO, usually an adhesion promoter in combination with a two-part epoxy or urethane adhesive. Hot-melt adhesives also work particularly well on TPOs due to their highly compatible formulation.

Conversely, neither cyanoacrylates nor methacrylates work well on TPO, even using the same adhesion promoters that work well for two-part adhesives. This seems to be mainly due to a chemical incompatibility between the acrylic composition of the adhesives and the polyolefin, but is also partly due to the fact that CAs and methacrylates tend to be much more rigid than TPOs. If the plastic flexes at all, the adhesive will tend to crack or pop off. Table 3.6 summarizes the pros and cons of the different repair methods on TPO.

In summary, the best repair methods for TPO are hot-melt adhesives, two-part adhesives, and fusion welding, in that order. Fusion welding may be preferred if a compatible welding rod can be found. Fusion welding may be the only option if part geometry precludes the use of adhesives.

Polyethylene

Like polypropylene and TPO, polyethylene is a polyolefin, or "oily" plastic. It is usually distinguishable by its greasy feel and waxy appearance. It is often molded in "natural" color, which

Table 3.6 - Repair Methods for TPO Parts

Repair Method	Comments
Two-Part Adhesives	May require the use of an adhesion promoter prior to application of repair material. Best on cracks, gouges, and holes.
Cyanoacrylate (CA)	CAs do not work on polyolefins such as TPO.
Hot-Melt	Hot-melts have excellent compatibility with TPO. Best on cracks and holes.
Methacrylate	Methacrylate adhesives do not work on polyolefins such as TPO.
Plastic Fusion Welding	Finding matching filler rod may be difficult. Best on cracks.

Table 3.7 - Repair Methods for Polyethylene Parts

Repair Method	Comments
Two-Part Adhesives	Two-parts do not stick well to polyethylene.
Cyanoacrylate (CA)	CAs do not work on polyolefins like PE.
Hot-Melt	Hot-melts stick well to PE but refinishing is a problem. Best on cracks and holes.
Methacrylate	Methacrylate adhesives do not work on PE.
Plastic Fusion Welding	This is the best way to repair polyethylene. Best on cracks and holes.

is a slightly translucent milky-white color. Even if it is molded in color, as it is on dirt bike and ATV fenders, it still appears waxy or partially translucent.

Unlike TPO, PE is most often molded in its straight, generic co-polymer form with few additives to modify physical properties. There are three major types of polyethylene, distinguished by their molecular structure: low-density polyethylene (LDPE), high-density polyethylene (HDPE), and linear low-density polyethylene (LLDPE). In this book, we will be most concerned with LDPE since that's the type that's most common on cars, trucks, motorcycles, and recreational vehicles. HDPE and LLDPE have more specialized applications and aren't as widely used in the transportation industry. When I refer to polyethylene, I'll mean LDPE unless I state otherwise.

Polyethylene is even more slippery than PP and TPO, making it virtually impossible for adhesive repair materials or paint to stick to it. Only certain hot-melt adhesives can make a lasting repair on polyethylene.

The best way to make a lasting repair on polyethylene is to fusion weld it with either an airless or hot-air welder. Because it has a fairly low softening point, PE is one of the easiest plastics to weld. For this reason, polyethylene parts make good candidates for repair if you're just learning how to repair plastics. Table 3.7 gives some rules of thumb for the types of damage each repair method is best suited for.

ABS

ABS, short for acrylonitrile butadiene styrene, is a very common plastic material used on many thousands of parts including automotive interiors, street bike fairings, and household appliances, just to name a few. Fortunately, it is also very easy to repair by a variety of methods. In fact, of all the repair methods I have categorized, only the hot-melt adhesive would be incompatible for repairing ABS.

There are two main reasons that ABS is simple to repair. First of all, it has a relatively high surface energy, meaning that adhesives will *wet out* on its surface well. If the adhesive can wet out on the surface, it can penetrate into all the microscopic nooks and crannies and actually lock itself into the part mechanically, creating much stronger adhesion.

The second reason ABS is easy to repair is that it is a rigid material. Generally, there are fewer repair options available for flexible materials because, in order for the repaired part to retain its functionality, the repair material must also have some flexibility. There are simply fewer flexible repair materials than there are rigid ones.

Because there are so many options open for the repair of ABS parts, the choice of repair method depends more on factors like part and damage geometry. Table 3.8 gives some rules of thumb as to what types of damage are best suited to each repair method.

Because so many different repair technologies work well on ABS, it's often best to use a "belt and suspenders" approach to the repair. Many times, a crack can be tacked together with CA, welded, and finally reinforced with a rigid epoxy on the backside. Using such procedures, the repair area can often be made to be stronger than the original material.

Polycarbonate and PC Blends

Polycarbonate is used in many of the same applications as ABS because it is also a rigid plastic, but PC has better strength and toughness than ABS. Naturally, it is also more expensive than ABS. General Electric markets polycarbonate under the trade name Lexan, which is a clear glazing material similar to acrylic but is much stronger and tougher.

In car and motorcycle applications, polycarbonate is usually blended with other plastics such as PBT (polyester) or ABS to modify engineering properties such as flexibility or thermal expansion coefficient. GE markets PC blends such as Pulse and Xenoy. Pulse is used on the door panels of Saturn automobiles and the fairings of some street bikes. Xenoy is used for bumper covers and reinforcements on some cars.

Polycarbonate is an easily weldable plastic and the blends can also usually be successfully welded using a straight PC filler rod. Welding is the best way to repair polycarbonate. PC has a high softening point so fusion welding will require a high heat level, but once the proper heat level is attained, PC melts and flows together very nicely. It is often helpful to preheat the area to be welded with a heat gun when using an airless welder. Preheating is not necessary when welding with a hot-air welder.

Because PC is rigid and has a relatively high surface energy, all adhesives work well with the exception of hot-melts, which are usually flexible. Two-part epoxies and urethanes are good for damage over large areas. CAs stick well to PC but shouldn't be used as the primary structural repair.

Table 3.8 - Repair Methods for ABS Parts	
Repair Method	**Comments**
Two-Part Adhesives	Best on cracks or large holes. Also use as backside reinforcement for welds or other repairs.
Cyanoacrylate (CA)	Best on tight-fitting cracks. If used with a tight-fitting backing plate, may make a good structural repair.
Hot-Melt	Not recommended, as most hot-melt adhesives are flexible.
Methacrylate	Best on missing tabs or flanges, cracks, or holes. Useful in areas where geometry is complicated.
Plastic Fusion Welding	Best on cracks. Difficult where geometry is complicated.

What's the Difference Between Peel and Shear Strength?

Many times, people who do a plastic repair will test the strength of the repair by picking at the edge of the adhesive in an attempt to peel it up. Even a repair that's perfectly done will often fail this extreme test. If the adhesive is peeled up, the verdict is usually that the repair material is "no good."

This test is not realistic in that it concentrates the forces in a single area whereas, in the real world, if a part is subjected to stress, the adhesive can spread the load out over a larger area. The figures here graphically demonstrate the concentration of force resulting from a peeling load.

The difference between peel and shear can be illustrated by a Band-Aid analogy. Most people peel their Band-Aids off from one edge. Placing the adhesive in peel concentrates the force along the line where the Band-Aid meets the skin, minimizing the amount of pain involved.

By contrast, if you were to grab the Band-Aid in the middle and yank the whole thing up at one time, it would take a lot more force (and result in a lot more pain!) to remove it. This kind of loading puts the adhesive on the Band-Aid in more of a shear load (there is an element of peel as the bandage raises away from the skin, however); the force is more evenly distributed over the entire area of the Band-Aid.

Peel loads are the most demanding for any adhesive joint. The peel strength depends on the flexibility and toughness of the adhesive itself and the surface energy of the substrate. Peel strength can be quite good in some instances—for example, a urethane two-part on a flexible thermoset urethane substrate. The urethane adhesive is tough and has very good adhesion to thermoset urethanes. Conversely, brittle adhesives, like cyanoacrylates, have almost no peel strength. And no matter what adhesive is used on a low-surface-energy substrate like TPO, the peel strength will be low.

A real-world strength test for a repaired joint would be to take the part in your hands and pull, twist, and flex the entire part over a range that it would be expected to withstand upon installation. If you were to bend the part backwards over on itself, you would probably succeed in destroying the repair, but it wouldn't represent the kind of loading the part would see in the real world except in another collision, at which point you would expect the part to break anyway. Having great peel strength would be desirable, but it's just impossible to achieve with current products over problematic substrates.

The moral of this story is: don't test your repair by trying to peel it up. As long as you do the surface preparation and application steps properly, you can usually determine if there will be a problem when you sand the adhesive back down. If the repair material feathers out on the substrate well, you probably have adequate adhesion and strength. If the sandpaper starts to peel the repair material up from the substrate at the featheredge, you don't have adequate adhesion. The second test would be to flex and bend the part over a range that's greater than what would be expected of it during and after installation. If the repair feathers out well and can withstand a fair amount of bending and flexing, you should feel confident in the quality of the repair. ■

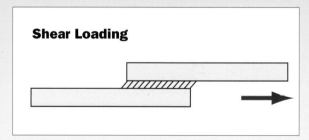

In shear loading, the force is distributed evenly over the adhesive area.

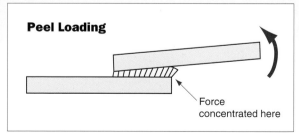

In peel loading, the entire force is concentrated at the edge of the adhesive. Once the edge fails, the rest of the adhesive joint will come undone like a zipper.

Table 3.9 - Repair Methods for Polycarbonate Parts

Repair Method	Comments
Two-Part Adhesives	Repair cracks, large holes, or gouges. Also use as backside reinforcement for welds.
Cyanoacrylate (CA)	Best on tight-fitting cracks, holes, or gouges. Good for tacking cracks together for repair by welding or two-part, but not recommended for structural repair.
Hot-Melt	Not recommended, as most hot-melt adhesives are flexible.
Methacrylate	Repair missing tabs or flanges, cracks, or holes. Useful in areas where geometry is complicated.
Plastic Fusion Welding	Cracks. Best way to repair cracks in polycarbonate.

Table 3.9 gives some rules of thumb as to which repair methods are best suited for various types of damage on polycarbonates.

To summarize, cracks in PC are best and most easily repaired by fusion welding, using either an airless or a hot-air welder. Damage over larger areas is best repaired using a two-part rigid epoxy, which is easier to sand than a urethane two-part. Finally, small tabs or flanges can be repaired with methacrylate adhesives.

Nylon and Nylon Blends

Polyamide, popularly known by the DuPont trade name Nylon, was invented by chemists at DuPont in 1939. It was first used as a fiber and became a hit product when it was used to replace silk in the manufacture of women's stockings. The bulk of nylon production today goes toward the textile industry, but there are also nylons designed for injection molding applications. Nylons are quite common on cars and motorcycles, particularly in high-temperature areas.

The most common application of nylon is for radiator tanks or end caps. All modern radiators are made from an aluminum heat exchanger capped at either end by injection molded, glass-reinforced nylon tanks, which are usually black in color. Nylon is chosen for this application because of its high heat resistance. Also, for this

same reason, nylon is the material of choice for plastic intake manifolds, valve covers, oil pans, and the like.

GE Plastics sells a popular nylon blend that is used with good success for vertical automotive body panels and motorcycle fairings. This material, which sells by the trade name GTX, is a blend of nylon and polyester. It is quite flexible yet still has good strength and toughness. GM uses it for the fenders and quarter panels on its Saturn line of cars, and VW uses it for the fenders on the new Beetle. As more vehicles move toward plastic vertical body panels, GTX is likely to be the material of choice for new applications.

Nylon and nylon blends, such as GTX, are easier to repair than polyolefins because they have a relatively high surface energy, which allows some adhesives to stick to them well. However, due to molecular structure incompatibilities, neither CAs nor methacrylate adhesives stick to nylon-based materials as well as they do to ABS or PC. For this reason, CAs and methacrylates are not the preferred repair option.

Fortunately, nylon is also an easily weldable material. In fact, welding is the only option for repair on underhood components such as radiator tanks. Nylon blends, such as GTX, can be successfully welded using a straight nylon welding rod. It is critical to thoroughly melt the nylon filler rod into the base material for a strong weld, however. This requires a high welding temperature. This process is aided by preheating the area to be welded with a high-temp heat gun.

Table 3.10 gives some rules of thumb as to which repair methods are best suited for various types of damage on nylon-based plastics.

To summarize, fusion welding is the best repair method for damage to nylon components. Two-part urethane or epoxy adhesives may also be used with success on body panels, but welding is the only choice for underhood components such as radiator tanks or intake manifolds.

PVC

PVC, also known as polyvinyl chloride or just plain vinyl, is an extremely common plastic, used for everything from children's toys to water pipe to seat covers. It is not very commonly used on automotive or motorcycle applications except

Table 3.10 - Repair Methods for Nylon-Based Parts	
Repair Method	**Comments**
Two-Part Adhesives	Use for cracks, holes, or gouges. Do not use on radiator tanks or other underhood components.
Cyanoacrylate (CA)	May be used for tacking cracks together for repair by welding or two-part, but not recommended for structural repair.
Hot-Melt	Not recommended, as most hot-melt adhesives are flexible.
Methacrylate	May be used for unstressed components.
Plastic Fusion Welding	Best repair method for cracks. Only way to repair underhood components like radiator tanks.

as an upholstery cover. For this reason, I won't delve deeply into the methods for repairing PVC, except for the sidebar on repairing dashboard covers in Chapter 4.

Like nylon, PVC may be repaired using adhesive or welding techniques. Two-part adhesives tend to stick well to PVC, as do CAs and methacrylates.

Fusion welding works very well, but precautions must be taken to avoid the fumes generated, *as they can be hazardous.* PVC sheet stock is often used to fabricate cabinets and such, and is easily and quickly welded with a hot-air welder. Airless fusion welding is also easy to do for repair work.

Because of PVC's inherent chemical instability, it may be dissolved or softened with the proper solvent blend. For this reason, one of the most common ways of joining PVC pipes is by solvent welding. To do this, solvent is simply wiped onto the surface, allowing the plastic on the surface to soften. The surfaces to be joined are pressed together, and the softened material on each surface co-mingles, creating a welded joint. The joint must be designed to allow one

part to lap over the other for a significant area, which occurs naturally when one pipe is slid inside another. In my years of experience in the field of plastic repair, I have never used a solvent weld, so I present it here more for academic than practical interest. It might be a useful technique if you are fabricating a structure from PVC sheet stock, but it is not likely to be useful for doing repairs.

Table 3.11 gives some rules of thumb as to which repair methods are best suited for various types of damage on PVC plastics.

Acrylic

Acrylic is the common name for polymethyl methacrylate (PMMA), the most important member of a range of acrylic polymers. They get their name because they are derivatives of acrylic acid. They were developed in the early twentieth century and, because of their excellent translucency, found their greatest use as replacements for glass glazing in aircraft. The most common trade names for the product are Plexiglas and Lucite.

Acrylic may be injection molded or extruded. Many common products are produced by manipulation of acrylic sheet, rod, or tube. Acrylic is not widely used on vehicular applications except for things like taillight lenses, headlight lenses, and windshields on street bikes — in other words, anywhere where translucency is important.

Table 3.11 - Repair Methods for PVC Parts	
Repair Method	**Comments**
Two-Part Adhesives	Sticks well, best for repairing large holes.
Cyanoacrylate (CA)	Good for tacking together tight-fitting cracks in preparation for repair with other method. Not recommended for structural repair.
Hot-Melt	Not recommended, as most hot-melt adhesives are flexible.
Methacrylate	Sticks well. May be used to fill holes and cracks.
Plastic Fusion Welding	PVC welds easily with airless or hot-air welder. Hot-air welder is faster when fabricating from sheet and pipe stock.

Repair Options Summary

		Two-Part Adhesives	Cyanoacrylate Adhesives	Hot Melt Adhesives	Methacrylate Adhesives	Fusion Welding
Thermoset	Fiberglass FRP, UP	✓ Best general purpose repair method	✓ Good on tight-fitting cracks		✓ Good for filling holes, restoring details	
	Sheet Molding Compound SMC	✓ Best general purpose repair method	✓ Good on tight-fitting cracks		✓ Good for filling holes, restoring details	
	Polyurethane PUR, RIM, RRIM	✓ Good for tears in flexible and rigid parts	✓ Good for tacking tears together	✓ Urethane hot melt good for tears in flexible parts.	✓ Good for restoring details on rigid parts	
	Dicyclopentadiene DCPD	✓ Best general purpose repair method	✓ Good on tight-fitting cracks		✓ Good for filling holes, restoring details	
Thermoplastic	Polypropylene & TPO PP, TPO, TEO, PP+EPDM	✓ May require adhesion promoter		✓ Best for tears, holes, and gouges		✓ Good if matching filler rod can be found
	Polyethylene PE, LDPE, HDPE			✓ Works, but refinishing difficult		✓ Best general purpose repair method
	Acrylonitrile Butadiene Styrene ABS	✓ Good for cracks, holes, and gouges	✓ Good for tacking cracks together		✓ Good for filling holes, restoring details	✓ Best for cracks
	Polycarbonate & blends PC, PC+PBT, PC+ABS	✓ Good for cracks, holes, and gouges	✓ Good for tacking cracks together		✓ Good for filling holes, restoring details	✓ Best for cracks
	Nylon & blends PA, PA+PPO	✓ Good for cracks, holes, and gouges	✓ Good for tacking cracks together		✓ Fair adhesion, restores details	✓ Best for cracks, radiator tanks
	Polyvinyl Chloride PVC (vinyl)	✓ Good for cracks, holes, and gouges	✓ Good for tacking cracks together		✓ Good for filling holes, restoring details	✓ Good for cracks
	Acrylic PMMA		✓ Good on tight-fitting cracks		✓ Best general purpose repair method	

Racing cars have long used Plexiglas glazing in place of glass as a weight reduction measure.

Though not suitable for repair work, acrylics are easily solvent welded as they are softened using solvents such as chloroform. Many times, fabrications of acrylic sheet and extruded angle are constructed using lap joints and solvent welds. Although acrylics are thermoplastic materials, they happen to be very difficult to weld due to their poor melt flow characteristics. Fortunately, they are easily repaired with most adhesives, especially with methacrylates.

Since translucency is an important feature of parts molded from acrylic, it follows that the repair material should also be transparent. For this reason, methacrylate adhesives are by far the best choice for the repair of acrylics. Not only can they be transparent, but they are also chemically identical to the acrylic material itself. In fact, methacrylate adhesives form an acrylic polymer when hardened. Cyanoacrylate adhesives also work well on tight-fitting cracks, but repairs made with CAs, particularly butt joints, may not withstand prolonged vibration or impact stress. Two-part adhesives also stick well to acrylic plastics, but they most often do not have the desired translucency.

Table 3.12 gives some rules of thumb as to which repair methods are best suited for various types of damage on acrylic plastics.

Other Thermoplastics

Although the plastic families previously discussed account for the vast majority of materials used in vehicular applications, there are other types of thermoplastics that may be used that don't fit into one of the above categories. The major resin manufacturers are constantly researching new blends and formulations to optimize certain properties that their customers desire. The field is in constant evolutionary motion, so this book can only provide a snapshot of the current technology. However, one or two decades from now, I suspect that the plastics used will still be largely similar to what we are using today.

If the plastic that you want to repair is a thermoplastic but does not fit neatly within one of the categories I have discussed, chances are it still may be repaired. If you have a plastic welder, the first thing to do is try a test weld using different welding rods. Pick two or three rods that most closely match the feel and appearance of the plastic you want to repair. Clean the plastic in an unexposed area and sand with coarse sandpaper. Melt a small patch of the welding rod onto the surface of the plastic and allow the filler rod to fuse together with the base material. Likewise, try the other plastic welding rods you have chosen. After these patches cool completely, try to pick them up with your fingernail. If the plastics are not compatible, the test weld should peel up very easily. If you're lucky, one of the plastic rods will stick so well you won't be able to peel it up at all. If that's the case, perform a fusion weld using this filler rod.

If none of the welding rods stick, all is not lost. Generally, as long as the plastic is not polyethylene, two-part adhesives should work. Most two-part repair materials have flexible or rigid formulations, so depending on the rigidity of the plastic you want to repair, select the proper adhesive and try it. Hot-melt adhesives are a good option if the plastic is semi-rigid, like a TPO. If it is a rigid plastic, depending on the type of damage, you might also try a CA or methacrylate adhesive.

Table 3.12 - Repair Methods for Acrylic Parts	
Repair Method	**Comments**
Two-Part Adhesives	Sticks well, but does not offer the desired translucency, in most cases.
Cyanoacrylate (CA)	Excellent for use in repairing tight-fitting cracks. May not stand up in the long run if part is subjected to stress or vibration unless joint can be designed in lap fashion.
Hot-Melt	Not recommended, as most hot-melt adhesives are flexible.
Methacrylate	Best repair method. Adhesive itself is translucent and butt joints can be beveled for long-lasting repairs. Chemistry of adhesive is perfectly compatible with base material.
Plastic Fusion Welding	Acrylic is difficult to impossible to weld. Not recommended.

When trying adhesives, it is not advisable to try the same peel test that I just recommended for testing welds. Peel strength is a weakness for any adhesive repair material used on plastic. Most adhesives are designed to be loaded in shear, so an adhesive that will perform a perfectly adequate repair in the real world may still be peeled up. The best test for an adhesive is to perform a full repair and test it in the real world. At the final step, if the repair material feathers out onto the plastic substrate when sanding with a dual action sander, you will most probably have a durable repair. If the repair material does not feather out well, you will most likely have to abandon the repair and buy a new replacement part.

The following table summarizes the recommended repair methods with pros and cons for each of the generic types of plastic.

Repair Procedures

Now that you've identified the plastic you're working with and determined the best way to repair it, it's time to get down to the actual repair process. The purpose of this chapter of the book is to guide you, step-by-step, through the entire repair process and to explain in detail how to perform repairs using each of the various methods.

Basic Repair and Refinishing Procedure

The entire process for repairing and refinishing plastics can be boiled down to five basic steps: Identify, Clean, Align, Repair, and Refinish. I've already discussed the Identify step at length. After identifying the plastic and the repair process, you need to clean the plastic thoroughly to prevent any contamination from causing adhesion problems for the repair or refinish materials. You then perform the repair you have selected, finish the repair cosmetically as necessary, and refinish.

A flowchart shows the entire repair process from the identification step to paint. This graphic provides an outline for this section of the book.

Clean the Plastic

Most plastic parts on cars, motorcycles, or recreational vehicles are constantly exposed to the elements. For example, a car's front bumper will probably have a layer of wax, a coating of dirt and tar, maybe some road salt, a few splattered bugs, and perhaps splatters of some other origin. And that's just on the outer surface. The inner surface will probably have mud splatters, oil spray, and maybe some transmission fluid drippings on it. Underhood plastics and street bike motorcycle fairings can be even more contaminated, especially with oil spray and drippings.

For a repair material or primer to have good adhesion on the plastic's surface, the plastic must first be cleaned. If the contaminates are left on the surface, it is more likely that the repair material will either stick to the contaminates themselves (dirt particles have a much higher surface energy than does any plastic) or not stick to anything at all. In engineering terms, adhesion is a *surface phenomenon*. In other words, adhesion between two materials is dependent on minute forces acting over molecular distances. One famous quote in the field that summarizes the frus-

Two-part adhesives are the most common method of repair for both thermosets and thermoplastics.

Basic Repair and Refinishing Procedure

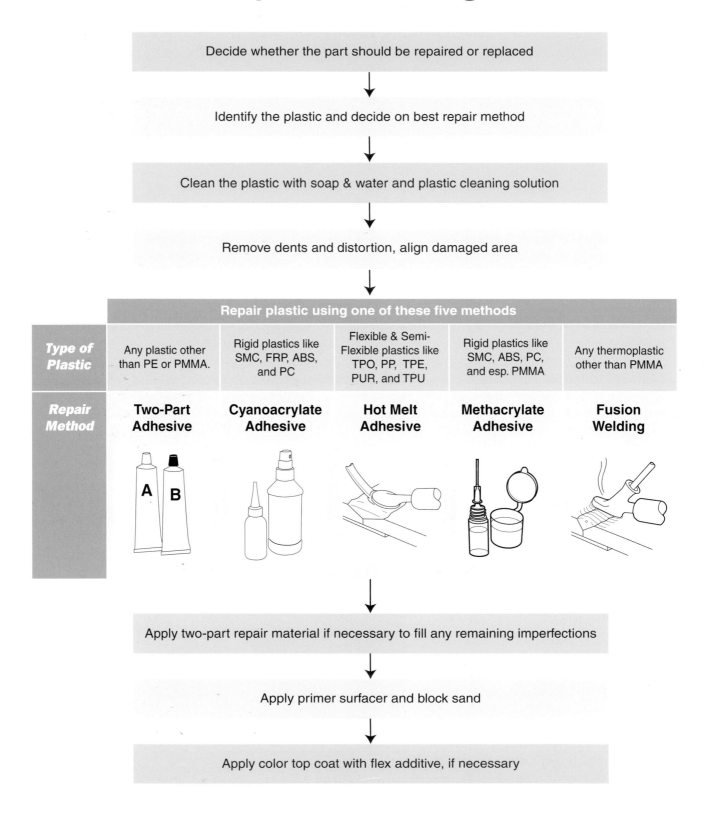

Decide whether the part should be repaired or replaced

↓

Identify the plastic and decide on best repair method

↓

Clean the plastic with soap & water and plastic cleaning solution

↓

Remove dents and distortion, align damaged area

↓

Repair plastic using one of these five methods				
Type of Plastic Any plastic other than PE or PMMA.	Rigid plastics like SMC, FRP, ABS, and PC	Flexible & Semi-Flexible plastics like TPO, PP, TPE, PUR, and TPU	Rigid plastics like SMC, ABS, PC, and esp. PMMA	Any thermoplastic other than PMMA
Repair Method Two-Part Adhesive	Cyanoacrylate Adhesive	Hot Melt Adhesive	Methacrylate Adhesive	Fusion Welding

↓

Apply two-part repair material if necessary to fill any remaining imperfections

↓

Apply primer surfacer and block sand

↓

Apply color top coat with flex additive, if necessary

tration that engineers have long had with adhesives is this: "God made solids, but surfaces were the work of the devil." Plastics, especially TPOs and polyolefins, are tough enough to repair without any surface contamination, so it is vital that you begin the repair process with a thorough cleaning of the surfaces.

First clean the surfaces with good old soap and water. Use a good dishwashing liquid detergent or one of the many plastic cleaning prep soaps available. Prep soaps have an advantage in that they usually have pumice or fine grit blended into the formulation that puts a fine sandscratch into the surface. This is especially helpful when doing an overall refinish on a part as it will aid in the adhesion of the first primer coat. For this reason, it is also a good idea to scrub the part with a scuff pad (like a 3M red Scotch-Brite pad). The scuff pad will also put a fine sandscratch into the surface, further aiding adhesion. After washing the part inside and out with soap and water, rinse all the soap and grit off with a liberal amount of clean water and let the part dry thoroughly.

Some surface contaminants, especially wax and grease, will resist removal by soap and water, so more aggressive means are necessary to remove them. This can be accomplished by using a solvent-based plastic cleaning solution. The solvents will dissolve these contaminates and take them into solution. As long as you wipe off the wet solvent before it evaporates, you will be able to completely remove these contaminants.

Most plastic repair product manufacturers make a plastic cleaning solution and most are used the same way. Working a small area at a time (say, a six-inch-diameter circle), spray on a heavy, wet coat of plastic cleaner directly onto the surface, wait for a couple of seconds, and wipe with a clean cloth. This process allows the contaminates to be dissolved into the cleaning solution, then wiped away and removed.

It is important to wipe the solvent off with a clean cloth in one direction only. Don't wipe the cloth back over the surface again or else you'll recontaminate the surface. You may rotate the cloth to expose a new, clean area, but the key is that each wipe should be with a clean surface of

Thermoplastics are characterized by the fact that they can be melted and resolidified. Because of this, they may be repaired using plastic welding techniques in addition to adhesive techniques.

the cloth in one direction only. If you notice that the cloth has picked up a heavy amount of contamination, you should repeat the cleaning process until the cloth is virtually unsoiled after it is wiped over the surface. Continue this process until the entire surface of the plastic part has been cleaned in this manner.

By following these procedures, the surface should be about as clean as is possible in a shop environment. Even though many repair materials are forgiving with regard to cleanliness, cleaning the surface by this procedure will definitely improve the chances for a successful repair and refinish, especially on low-surface-energy plastics like polyolefins. Once you've got the plastic cleaned and all surfaces are as near to their virgin state as possible, you're ready to tackle the actual repair process.

The only exception to the rule of cleaning before repairing is on SMC. When SMC breaks, there is glass fiber and talc exposed at the raw edge of the panel. If water or a cleaning solvent is applied, it will wick right into the panel by capillary action, possibly damaging the structure of the material. The best way to repair a broken SMC panel is to first fit the broken edges together as closely as possible, allowing the fibers to intertwine, then soak the broken area with a thin cyanoacrylate adhesive. The thin adhesive will wick into all the nooks and crannies and create the basis for a very strong repair.

Align the Damage

Before you proceed with the repair process, you must first align the damage together as closely as possible. Many times when plastics, especially more flexible plastics like TPO, suffer impact damage, they not only tear but they also distort as well. Rigid plastics tend to crack or shatter, not bend and distort.

If the plastic is distorted, it needs to be bent back into shape or ground away before you proceed with the repair. Most plastics can be softened with heat and forced back into position. Thermoplastics can be reshaped this way. Even thermoset polyurethane, often used for flexible bumper covers, can recover its original shape if heated. Only SMC and FRP cannot be reshaped with heat; any distorted areas on these plastics will have to be ground or cut away.

When reshaping a distorted area on a thermoplastic part, the best tool to have is a high-temp heat gun. With the heat on the highest temperature setting, carefully and slowly heat the distorted area on one side only. Move the heat gun around; be careful not to get too close or hold the hot air over one area too long. Keep heating the plastic until it becomes too uncomfortable to touch on the opposite side. If you do this, you can be assured that the plastic is heated thoroughly all the way through. If you heat from both sides, it may be uncomfortable to the touch on the outer surfaces, but may still be too cool in the middle. Be patient with this process; it could take several minutes.

Once the plastic is heated all the way through, put the heat gun down and immediately push the softened plastic back into shape with a tool like a wooden block or a screwdriver handle. If you wear gloves, you can also use your hands to help shape the plastic. Work quickly as the plastic will get stiffer as it cools down. Once you have the plastic back in shape, immediately quench it with a wet cloth.

Reshaping a distorted area on a thermoset polyurethane part is often easier. Because of the crosslinks that form between the molecules in urethane, the material has a "memory." In other words, when heated, the molecules can move and realign themselves into their original positions. As a result, the distortion may pop back into place all by itself without your having to push it. By contrast, thermoplastics don't have a memory and are just as happy to be in their newly distorted configuration. That's why you have to manually force a thermoplastic part back into place.

Thermoset urethanes may be heated with a heat gun in the distorted area alone, or the entire part may be heated at one time. There are a few ways to do this. Many bumper recycling companies will use a large tank of water kept at about 180 degrees F. Most distortions in the part are removed by dipping the entire part into the water for 10 to 20 minutes. Body shops with a heated spray booth can achieve the same effect by putting the part in the booth for a while. Urethane parts can even come back to shape if set out in the direct sunlight on a hot day for some time.

Depending on the repair method you choose, you may also tape or clamp the crack together at this point. Most often, however, it's better to leave the crack open while you prepare for the adhesive or weld repair as it makes it easier to grind in the V-groove and verify its depth if you can pry the crack apart. Usually it's best to tape or clamp the frontside of the repair after the backside has been ground and prepared.

Introduction to Adhesives

The most common technique for repairing plastics is the use of adhesives. For the most part, they don't require any special equipment for their use other than perhaps a cartridge gun. Ad-

Before You Do Anything Else, Clean the Plastic!

If you start sanding on the plastic before you clean it, you'll embed all the junk that's on the surface right into the plastic, possibly causing you adhesion problems down the line. If you want to do the job right, clean the plastic first before you dive into the repair! ∎

1. Rinse the part off with water. Using a dishwashing detergent or an abrasive plastic cleaning soap, thoroughly clean both the inner and outer surfaces of the plastic. If you are just going to refinish in the repair area and blend into the original, use a non-abrasive soap. Don't use an abrasive soap unless you're planning to refinish the part all over. If you are doing a panel refinish, scrubbing the soap with a scuff pad (3M Red, for example) will give you more aggressive scratches for better primer adhesion. Once you've finished washing, rinse again to remove all soap residue and allow to dry.

2. Spray a heavy, wet coat of a plastic cleaning solution onto the surface in a small area (say six- to nine-inch-diameter circle). Allow the solvent to sit for a few seconds to allow any contamination to be taken into solution.

3. Before the solvent evaporates, wipe it off in one direction with a clean, dry cloth. For each subsequent wipe, turn the cloth so that a clean, dry surface is always exposed to the plastic. If you backwipe or wipe with an already used surface, you will be transferring contaminates from the cloth back onto the surface. Repeat the above process until the entire part has been cleaned.

Align the Damage Prior to Repair

1. On thermoplastic or flexible thermoset urethane parts, heat the distorted area with a heat gun from one side only. Hold the heat gun back and keep it moving to keep from overheating the plastic. Be patient and continue heating until the opposite side of the part is too hot to touch. This way you know the plastic is heated all the way through.

2. Once the plastic is heated, force the distorted area back into shape with a tool (such as a wood block or screwdriver handle) or a gloved hand. Work quickly as the plastic will stiffen as it cools off.

3. When the plastic has been forced back into shape, immediately quench both sides with water.

hesives are especially convenient for the occasional repair as there is no up-front investment in equipment like there is for doing plastic welding repairs. The cost of the material is a bit higher than it is for welding, but that's the trade-off for convenience. Furthermore, adhesives are generally very easy to use.

In this chapter, I'll guide you through the repair process for each of the four major types of adhesives used in plastic repair: two-parts, cyanoacrylates, hot-melts, and methacrylates. Within the two-part category, there are several different types of adhesives. I'll discuss the pros and cons of each so you can decide what's best for your application.

Repair with Two-Part Adhesives

In body shops around the world, by far the most common products used in plastic repair are two-part adhesive materials. They get their name from the fact that they consist of two components, commonly called an *A Side and B Side,* or *Resin and Hardener.* The separate components are liquid or paste until mixed together in the proper proportions. When mixed, a chemical reaction begins that will result in the material becoming solidified. In other words, a two-part adhesive is, in itself, simply a thermoset plastic.

A specially formulated thermoset plastic, that is. The adhesive must have the proper balance of open time (working time), cure time, viscosity, strength, flexibility, adhesion, sandability, and durability to work effectively. That's why there are many different types of two-parts available. There's bound to be one designed for the job you need to do.

I'll first discuss the four generic types of two-part repair materials available and the pros and cons of each to help you choose the right one for the job at hand. After that, I'll show you how to perform both structural and cosmetic repairs with two-part adhesives.

Two-Part Adhesives: Four Types

The four generic types of two-part adhesives available for doing plastic repairs are epoxies, urethanes, acrylics, and polyesters. Most people who've had any experience with bodywork are familiar with polyester fillers. These are commonly called Bondo (which is a trademark of the Bondo/Mar Hyde Corporation), but are generically called *body fillers*. Polyester body filler is not usually recommended for plastic repair, but it does have its place. I'll discuss polyester fillers later in this chapter.

More common for plastic repair are epoxy and urethane two-parts. Epoxies are easier to sand than urethane, but aren't quite as strong. Urethanes are very strong and tough, but due to this characteristic, they are also hard to sand. One company, Lord Corporation, makes an acrylic-based two-part repair material that competes in this category. I'll discuss each in turn.

Table 4.1 lists flexible and rigid plastic repair products made by the major automotive plastic repair product manufacturers.

Epoxy Two-Part Materials Epoxies are the most popular two-part plastic repair material for good reason: they are easy to work with, they offer a wide range of physical properties, and they have great sandability. Epoxy can be formulated to offer flexibility or rigidity to match any substrate from soft urethanes to rigid SMCs. Epoxy's open time can be adjusted anywhere between five minutes and 60 minutes and its viscosity can be adjusted fairly high to enable the uncured product to hang onto a vertical panel. Finally, one of epoxy's greatest strengths is its excellent sandability. This is an important characteristic when you're trying to achieve an "invisible" repair.

Epoxy is stronger than less-expensive polyester systems, but not as strong as the more expensive urethane two-part systems. Although epoxies can make a perfectly adequate structural repair on most plastics, urethanes will generally have the edge on epoxies with regard to strength. However, since most plastic parts are not subject to a great amount of stress, the strength of epoxy will be more than adequate in virtually every situation.

Repair materials generally fall into one of four categories: flexible fast cure, semi-rigid fast cure, rigid fast cure, and rigid slow cure. Because repair cycle time is important in the professional environment, fast cure products are usually preferred. The only time that you would

Table 4.1 - Two-Part Repair Materials			
Manufacturer	**Flexible, Fast Cure**	**Rigid, Fast Cure**	**Rigid, Slow Cure**
Crest Industries	TE-F	TE-R	BC-IB
Dominion Sure Seal	4008	4006	4025
Duramix	4030	4050	4950
International Epoxies	8010	8001	621
Lord Fusor	105/106	102	200
Proform	PF704	PF702	PF725-2
Protech	EF456	EF452	
Rubber Seal	RS-704-5	RS-720	RS-131
SEM	3992	3976	3931
3M	05887	05885	08115
Urethane Supply	2000	2020	2035

typically want to use a slow cure product is when you are bonding a panel onto a vehicle, that is, whenever you need to lay down a long bead of adhesive which may take some time to attach and clamp into position.

If you are repairing plastic for the first time, an epoxy two-part is likely to be your best bet on virtually any kind of plastic. Polyolefin substrates will present a challenge with regard to adhesion, but most work satisfactorily as long as an adhesion promoter is used first.

Epoxy chemistry is also used to create a clear resin, which is used in a manner similar to polyester resin for the creation of composite structures like FRP (fiberglass). Epoxy resins are more expensive than polyester resins but provide greater strength. Straight epoxy resin doesn't have any fillers or additives to modify its properties and make it easy to use as a repair material, However, epoxy resin also has its place in making repairs, but more often on boats and airplanes that are made of FRP as opposed to cars and motorcycles, which typically don't use FRP components.

Urethane Two-Part Materials

Urethane two-parts are not as common as epoxies because their chemistry is more complex and thus more difficult to formulate and manufacture. Polymer Engineering Corporation pioneered the use of urethane two-parts for automotive plastic repair in the late 1980s and since then other companies have introduced similar products.

Two-part repair materials made from polyurethane chemistry are basically the same as the two-part polyurethane that is used to make flexible bumper covers and the like. The repair materials differ with respect to the additives used to impart special properties such as sandability, but their chemistry is very much the same as that of the material used to make to original part. Therefore, urethane two-parts are an excellent choice for repairing thermoset urethane parts due to their compatibility with the substrate.

Urethane's primary advantage over epoxy is strength, especially on flexible repairs. By adjusting the frequency of crosslinks between molecule chains, manufacturers can adjust polyurethane stiffness anywhere from brick-like hardness to dead soft rubber. The system can therefore be engineered to provide just the right amount of stiffness. The crosslinked structure of the urethane system has excellent "memory," that is, after it deforms, it tends to return to its original position. This makes the repair material very tough and able to withstand deformation.

Because of this toughness, urethane adhesives also exhibit very good peel strength, or resistance to being peeled up. Assuming that the substrate is one to which the adhesive can bond well (thermoset urethane or metal, for example), urethane will be much stronger in peel than any other adhesive. Although most repairs and bonded joints are designed to be loaded in shear, not peel, it is reassuring to know that urethane's strength is there in case it is needed.

The flip side of urethane's toughness and strength is its generally poor sandability. On a microscopic level, the process of sanding is a machining process where the small, hard particles embedded in the sandpaper rub over the surface and remove chips of the substrate. Because the polyurethane matrix is so tough and strong, it takes more time for sandpaper to machine it.

Whereas epoxy chemistry allows the use a high level of mineral fillers to enhance sandability, urethane chemistry typically does not, further reducing its sandability in comparison with epoxy.

Other disadvantages of urethane adhesives compared to epoxies is that they are generally messier, they have to be used in a special cartridge gun, they have a shorter shelf life, and they contain potentially hazardous chemicals. The viscosity of the A- and B-sides of a urethane adhesive is lower than that of epoxy, which makes for a stringy, gooey mess when something goes wrong in the application process. Unlike epoxies, which can be squeezed out on a board individually and mixed by hand, urethane adhesives are packed exclusively in dual-mix packages that use a static mixer tip and a special cartridge gun. Unless you will be doing a lot of plastic repairs, the cost of this special cartridge gun will likely persuade you to use another type of adhesive. Unlike epoxies, urethanes are sensitive to moisture in the air, and thus have a shorter shelf life than do epoxies. Finally, two-part urethanes contain isocyanates, which have been proven to cause physical problems for those exposed to it for a long period of time. Realistically though, the amount of exposure to isocyanate in doing the occasional plastic repair would be negligible and wouldn't likely be a problem unless one was already sensitized to the chemical.

One final problem that has been exhibited with polyurethane adhesives for repair use is their tendency to *gas off* after the cure is completed. What typically happens is that the repair will be finished, sanded, and painted. After some time, bubbles may form under the paint film. These result from vapors created by the urethane adhesive during its curing process being trapped underneath the paint. This problem is exhibited to a greater or lesser degree depending on the manufacturer of the product.

Like epoxies, urethane repair materials generally fall into one of four categories: flexible fast cure, semi-rigid fast cure, rigid fast cure, and rigid slow cure. Although I won't cover them in this book, urethanes can also be formulated into a wide variety of other products, including flowable seam sealers and expanding foams.

Structural Repairs with Two-Part Adhesives

1. After cleaning and aligning the plastic, grind the plastic on the backside with coarse sandpaper (36- to 80-grit). If the repair on the backside has to be sanded flush, then V-groove the plastic on the backside about one inch wide. If you can leave a buildup on the backside, however, you can make a stronger repair. In that case, simply grind the plastic without V-grooving. Scratch the plastic up thoroughly anywhere you plan to apply adhesive, and then some. Blow the area dust-free.

2. To minimize the need for cosmetic filler on the frontside of the plastic, tape the cracked plastic together on the frontside so that the outer surface is lined up. Stiff aluminum-backed body tape is best for this. If the plastic is not polyolefin, an instant cyanoacrylate glue can also be used to hold the broken pieces together. Clamps or baling wire can also be used to hold the broken pieces in alignment while you apply the adhesive to the backside.

3. If aluminum body tape is used to align the tear on the frontside, use a plastic body spreader to press it firmly to the surface. This will help assure proper alignment when the repair material on the backside cures.

4. If the substrate is polyolefin, an adhesion promoter may be necessary to help the repair material to stick. Read the instructions for the repair material to see if this step is necessary. If so, apply the adhesion promoter and allow the solvents to flash off according to product instructions. Wait for the prescribed time before applying the repair material.

5. If the repair material recommends the use of a fiberglass cloth or open weave tape, cut it to size before mixing the adhesive. Cut the tape or cloth to overlap the damage at least one inch on each side of the crack or hole.

(cont. on next page)

To summarize, a urethane two-part is an excellent choice in doing repairs on thermoset urethane parts or on anything where optimum peel strength and toughness are desired. To minimize problems that result from urethane's poor sandability and its propensity to gas off, some technicians will use a urethane adhesive only on the backside of the repair for strength and an epoxy on the frontside for sandability.

Acrylic Two-Part Materials Although not common, for the sake of completeness, I will review a two-part material using acrylic chemistry. Lord Corporation, a large supplier of adhesives to automotive OEMs and other industries, sells a

Structural Repairs with Two-Part Adhesives (Cont.)

6. Mix the adhesive according to product instructions.

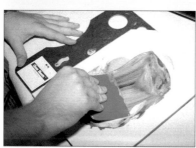

7. If packaged in individual squeeze tubes, dispense the appropriate amount on a mixing board and mix thoroughly until the color of the putty is uniform. If using a cartridge with a static mixer tip, dispense according to the directions.

8. After mixing the two-part repair material according to product instructions, immediately apply a smooth, even layer of repair material to the prepared area with a body spreader.

9. If you are inserting a fiberglass cloth or tape reinforcement, do it immediately after applying the first layer of repair material. Position it into the adhesive and press it slightly into the material to keep it locked in position.

line of aftermarket repair products under the Fusor brand name. Most of their products use epoxy formulations, but their bumper repair material (part numbers 105 and 106) uses an acrylic formulation.

The product is unusual in that its mixing ratio is 2:1 instead of the normal 1:1. It is distinguishable by its unusual smell and the fact that the diameter of one cartridge is smaller than the other. Like a urethane adhesive, Fusor 105 must be applied using a dual-mix pack, static mixer tip, and a special cartridge gun. The product is much more easily sandable than a urethane, however, and is similar to an epoxy in this regard.

10. Apply another even coating of repair material over the reinforcement while the adhesive is still wet. Allow the adhesive on the backside to harden before continuing the repair process on the frontside.

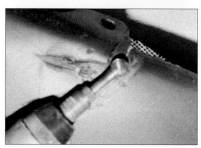

11. Remove the fixturing tape or clamps from the part. Using a high-speed die grinder, remove plastic along the crack to create a V-groove. A wider V-groove is preferable for maximum strength (3/4 to 2 inches total width). If you V-grooved the backside, then the frontside V-groove should go deep enough to meet the repair material on the backside. If the backside was not V-grooved, grind the frontside V-groove all the way through the plastic.

12. Scratch the plastic inside the V-groove with coarse sandpaper (36- to 80-grit). Completely remove any evidence of shiny plastic that remains from the die grinding stage. Ideally, all of the plastic inside the V-groove should be evenly sandscratched.

13. Round off the edge of the V-groove and transition to the surrounding area using 80-grit paper in a DA sander. Feather back the paint surrounding the V-groove with the 80-grit. Finally, scratch the paint for an area about one inch outside the V-groove with 180-grit paper in a DA. Blow the area dust-free with clean, dry compressed air.

(cont. on next page)

Structural Repairs with Two-Part Adhesives (Cont.)

14. If the substrate is polyolefin, an adhesion promoter may be necessary to help the repair material to stick. Read the instructions for the repair material to see if this step is necessary. If so, apply the adhesion promoter and allow the solvents to flash off according to product instructions. Wait for the prescribed time before applying the repair material.

15. Mix and apply the repair material into the V-groove on the frontside. Crown the material slightly to allow it to be sanded back flush in the finishing stage. Wait the prescribed amount of time before sanding. For better featheredging, allow as much time as possible for the repair material to cure when working on TPO substrates.

16. Rough contour and feather out the repair material with 80-grit in either a block sander or a DA. If working on a TPO, switch to 120- or 180-grit before you begin featheredging the material out onto the surface.

17. Any remaining low spots in the repair will have a smooth, shiny appearance since they have not been touched with the sandpaper. Before applying any more filler on these spots, first sandscratch these low spots lightly with a coarse sandpaper to remove any glossiness.

18. Mix and apply another coat of filler to fill the remaining low spots. Repeat the process to fill remaining low spots. When repair area is filled to your satisfaction, finish sand the area smooth with 180- or 220-grit sandpaper before proceeding to the refinishing step.

Polyester Two-Part Materials Like epoxies, polyester systems are available as a straight, clear resin for creating FRP (fiberglass) composite structures or as a modified system more suitable for doing repair work. The clear resin may be used for doing repairs on fiberglass boat hulls and the like, but its poor sandability and low viscosity limit its application for doing repair work.

Polyester-based repair materials are the most widely used plastic-based adhesives used in the autobody industry, although not for plastic repair. Polyester body fillers, commonly called Bondo, are the materials of choice for smoothing out dents in metal body panels. Body fillers are polyester resins modified with mineral fillers and other additives to keep it from sagging on vertical surfaces and to improve its sandability.

Unlike most other two-parts that are mixed in a 1:1 or 2:1 ratio, polyester resins and fillers are catalyzed using only a small amount of hardener. The catalyst usually contains MEK peroxide or benzoyl peroxide, which kicks off the chemical reaction between the polymeric and monomeric components of the polyester resin. For fillers, the catalyst is usually a paste called *cream hardener,* and is colored red or blue. The paste is squeezed out in proper proportion on top of a scoop of the resin and mixed in completely until the color of the finished material is uniform without streaks.

Polyester body fillers are not commonly used as structural repair materials, only as cosmetic fillers. Because of their high mineral content, they tend to be brittle when loaded in tension. They are also quite rigid, so if subjected to flex, they will either debond from the substrate or simply crack. They are mainly intended for cosmetic filling, and they work very well in that role because of their extremely good sandability.

Because they are rigid, polyester fillers are not usually recommended for use on plastics as most plastic substrates are at least somewhat flexible. The only exceptions would be for extremely rigid plastics like FRP, SMC, and polycarbonate. Polyester fillers can be used with confidence on these types of plastics as a cosmetic filler.

Structural Repair with Two-Part Adhesives

Whether you use a rigid two-part epoxy or urethane adhesive, the preparation method and use of each is about the same. The basic rules of plastic repair surface preparation are as follows: clean the surface and abrade it. Cleaning will remove contaminates that may prevent the adhesive from sticking to the surface. Abrading the

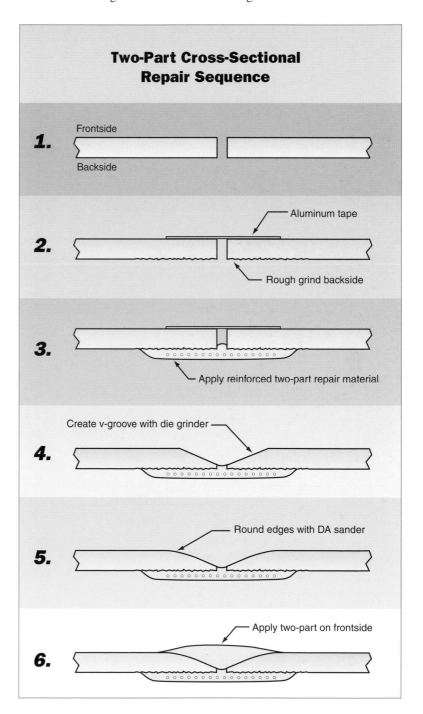

Two-Part Cross-Sectional Repair Sequence

1. Frontside / Backside

2. Aluminum tape / Rough grind backside

3. Apply reinforced two-part repair material

4. Create v-groove with die grinder

5. Round edges with DA sander

6. Apply two-part on frontside

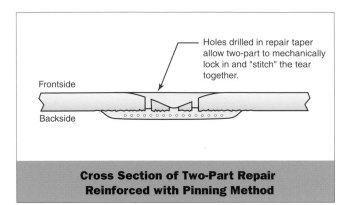

Holes drilled in repair taper allow two-part to mechanically lock in and "stitch" the tear together.

Frontside

Backside

Cross Section of Two-Part Repair Reinforced with Pinning Method

surface with sandpaper will increase the surface area for the adhesive to stick to. Both steps are critical to creation of a strong, reliable repair.

Abrade and V-Groove the Plastic   I've already covered the cleaning step earlier in this chapter. After you've cleaned the plastic, abrade the backside, or non-cosmetic side, of the plastic with coarse sandpaper, somewhere in the range of 36- to 80-grit. Very coarse sandpaper will put deep, heavy grooves in the surface and to some extent will allow the adhesive to lock in mechanically. Even if you sand with a 24- to 36-grit paper, it's still a good idea to sand the area with 80-grit to further increase the total surface area available for the adhesive to stick to.

You may choose to V-groove into the substrate or grind it flat. If you cannot build up a reinforcing patch on the backside due to space limitations or appearance considerations, you will need to grind a V-groove into the plastic. If you can build up a reinforcing layer on the backside, you will achieve a stronger repair. In this case, it's not necessary to V-groove into the backside, simply grind the plastic flat. This will allow you to have an even deeper V-groove on the frontside for added strength.

If the cosmetic appearance of the part is not important on either side of the plastic, it is best to V-groove halfway through on both sides and to build up a reinforcing layer on both sides to overlap the outer edges of the V-groove. Such construction can create a repair that is stronger than the original material.

If you decide to V-groove into the backside, it is helpful to first remove the plastic using a die grinder or Dremel tool. The depth of the V-groove should be about halfway through the plastic. The width of the V-groove depends on the amount of strength you require. A wider V-groove will expose more surface area to the adhesive, making for a stronger repair. A narrow V-groove will be sufficient for areas where you expect there will be no stress. In either case, your V-groove should range between 3/8 and 2 inches (10 to 50mm) wide.

Remove the Dust   Once you've got a good scratch on the surface and you've completely removed the shine, remove the sanding dust and chips. The best way to do this is to blow it off with a blow gun and a source of clean, dry, compressed air. Be careful not to recontaminate the surface by blowing oily or wet compressed air onto the part. If in doubt, just wipe off the sanding dust with a clean cloth. Wiping the dust off won't remove as much dust as a blast of compressed air, but at least you don't have to worry about contaminating the surface, which will cause even bigger problems.

At this stage, some plastic repair manufacturers recommend cleaning the plastic again with a plastic cleaning solution. This is okay to do as long as you allow enough time for the solvents to completely evaporate. The problem is that once you've sanded all these microscopic nooks and crannies in the surface of the plastic, reapplying the cleaning solvents will allow the solvent's molecules to tuck themselves away deep within the sandscratches. These solvents may create adhesion problems and may cause the repair to bubble up when they try to evaporate.

Even though the plastic appears to be dry after wiping, the unevaporated solvents may still be hiding away within these sandscratches. Allowing 10 to 15 minutes of evaporation time, or heating the area slightly with a high-temp heat gun should be sufficient to ensure that all the cleaning solvent has evaporated.

In contrast, some plastic repair manufacturers recommend that you not apply a cleaning solvent after the sanding step in order to avoid this problem. As long as the plastic was cleaned prior to sanding and as long as clean sandpaper was used to abrade the surface, there should not have been any opportunity for the surface to become con-

Strengthening Two-Part Adhesive Repairs with the Pinning Method

Some two-part adhesive manufacturers recommend a special procedure to strengthen repairs, called *pinning*. This involves drilling small holes (1/8- to 3/16-inch diameter) through the plastic in the repair taper along both sides of the tear. This allows adhesive to seep into the holes during application. Once the repair material cures, the material in the holes enhances the ultimate strength of the repair. If the repair were to be placed in tension, the material that has locked into the holes can provide greater resistance to the stresses applied. In other words, the repair doesn't have to rely solely on the adhesive bond between the base material and the substrate. ∎

1. Grind a V-groove (or repair taper) into plastic using a high-speed die grinder and appropriate bit. The repair taper should be at least 1-1/2 inches wide. The pinning method often works best when you prepare both sides before applying any adhesive. This allows you to drill completely through the plastic.

2. Drill a series of small holes well inside the repair taper along the length of the tear. The holes should be 1/8- to 3/16- inch in diameter. The holes should be spaced 1/2- to 3/4-inch apart for maximum effectiveness.

3. Grind the plastic with coarse sandpaper (36- to 80-grit) at low speed with an electric rotary sander. Round off the edges of the V-groove and sand out onto the surrounding area with 80-grit in a DA. Blow dust-free.

4. Apply two-part repair material over the repair taper, forcing adhesive into the holes. Once the adhesive cures, the repair can resist stress by mechanical as well as adhesive means.

Using Static Mixer Tips with Two-Part Adhesives

Static mixer tips are great for applying long beads of adhesive to a surface. Properly used, they also ensure a proper mix ratio between the two sides of the adhesive. Their use requires a little preparation, however, which I'll review here. ∎

1. First remove the plugs from the nozzle end of the cartridges. There are different designs depending on the manufacturer, but for most, simply unscrew the nut at the nozzles and pry out the plugs. Using a sharp steel T-pin or nail, make sure the nozzles are open and not clogged with hardened material. This is a particular problem with urethane two-part adhesives.

2. Load the cartridge in the gun, but don't install the mixer tip yet. Dispense a small amount of material onto a board until both sides begin to flow smoothly, evenly, and equally. The purpose of this is to balance the volume in each side. If one side is flowing more volume than the other (assuming it's a 1:1 ratio adhesive), check the nozzle again with the T-pin to make sure there's no blockage.

3. Install the mixer tip and screw on the nut that keeps it in place. Make sure you use the mixer tip supplied by the adhesive's manufacturer. Mixer tips come in many different lengths. If the tip is too short, you won't get proper mixing. If the tip is too long, too much effort will be required to squeeze it out. If the outlet of the tip is stepped, cut the opening to match the size of bead you want to make. A larger outlet will result in less effort to squeeze it out.

4. Before applying adhesive to the repair area, first squeeze a small amount out of the mixer tip onto a board. Verify that the color of the bead is uniform with minimal streaking. The pistons in both sides of the cartridge should advance evenly with firm pressure at the gun. If everything looks and feels good, begin immediately to apply adhesive to the repair area.

taminated. (That is, as long as your hands are also clean! Don't eat pizza while you're repairing plastic!) Simply blow the surface dust-free and continue to the next step.

Pinning Method

Some plastic repair manufacturers recommend a process called *pinning* to maximize the mechanical strength of the repair. In this process, a series of small holes (1/8- to 3/16- inch) are drilled in the repair taper. These holes will allow the adhesive to seep into them, mechanically locking the adhesive into the substrate. Testing has shown that this method will improve ultimate strength, so use it if you would like that extra edge in the strength department. Most often, plastic parts are not heavily stressed during use and usually crack due to impact, so this pinning step may be superfluous in most cases.

Prior to applying the adhesive on the backside of the part, make sure the parts are in position and aligned properly. You may have had to heat the plastic in order to remove any distortions and get the parts to line back up. Align the parts by tacking them with cyanoacrylate glue, taping them with an aluminum-backed tape, or by clamping them together.

Apply Adhesion Promoter if Necessary

If the substrate is a polyolefin like polypropylene, polyethylene, or TPO, consider using another method for doing a structural repair. Two-part adhesives usually don't exhibit the best adhesion to these substrates, so another repair method will likely give you better results. Sometimes, however, the use of two-parts on these substrates is unavoidable, so you'll want to follow the manufacturer's recommendations regarding the use of an adhesion promoter.

Adhesion promoters are not normally required on plastics other than polyolefins. If the substrate is polyolefin, most plastic repair product manufacturers recommend a coating of adhesion promoter before application of the adhesive. Some two-part repair materials are formulated such that they don't require an adhesion promoter, however. If required, the adhesion promoter is typically sprayed or brushed onto the surface. It usually takes five to ten minutes for solvents in the adhesion promoter to flash off (evaporate) and for the resin to set.

Prepare Reinforcing if Necessary

When doing structural repairs on rigid or flexible plastics with a two-part material, most manufacturers recommend that you reinforce the repair, at least on the backside, with fiberglass cloth or an open-weave fiberglass tape. To do this, you'll need to prepare your reinforcement material before you apply the adhesive.

Simply cut the tape or cloth to the size that will overlap the damage at least one inch on each side of the crack or hole. When you apply the reinforcement, it is best to encase it within the adhesive rather than apply it directly to the back of the plastic. Some manufacturers suggest that you should apply the strip of the fiberglass tape directly to the back of the plastic then cover it with the adhesive. This is easy to do, but it sacrifices much of the fiberglass's capability to reinforce the repair. By burying the fiberglass between layers of adhesive, you are creating a composite structure that will be much stronger due to the ability of the fiberglass to take tensile stresses.

To encase the fiberglass reinforcement within the adhesive: first, lay down a layer of adhesive; then lay the reinforcement on top of it while it is wet; and apply another layer of adhesive onto the first, again while the first layer of adhesive is still wet. Open-weave fiberglass tape (like drywall tape) is easy to bury in as the adhesive will flow very easily between the open strands. If you use fiberglass mat or cloth to reinforce, you'll also need a saturation roller to work the adhesive in between the strands of the fiberglass cloth. To do this with minimum mess, put down a layer of polyethylene film (like Saran Wrap) on top of the epoxy, and then work the adhesive into the mat with a saturation roller. Leave the plastic film on the epoxy until it cures, then peel it off.

Mix and Apply the Adhesive

Two-part repair materials require a thorough mixing of the two components in order for the molecules in the adhesive to intermingle and thus cure properly. Depending on the type of adhesive used, there are two ways to do this. First, you can mix the two components by hand on a mixing board. Second, you can use some automatic means of mixing the two components, like a static mixer tip on a cartridge package.

Epoxy adhesives are more forgiving than urethanes in that they allow the use of either hand mixing or automatic mixing. Urethane adhesive manufacturers recommend against hand mixing. Acrylic adhesives are not typically 1:1 mix ratios, so they would be more difficult to hand mix. Finally, polyester fillers are always hand mixed, but they shouldn't be used on a structural repair.

If you apply the adhesive by hand, squeeze out the appropriate amount of material onto a clean mixing board in the proper proportions (usually 1:1). Mix with a spatula, paint stick, or body spreader. To minimize the amount of air entrained into the mixture, it is best to use a body spreader and spread the mixture out on the board as you mix it, to expose any air bubbles and pop them during the process. The individual components of two-part adhesives are always of a different color, so you can tell when the mixing is complete. Simply continue mixing until there are no more streaks and the putty becomes a uniform color.

If you use a cartridge with a static mixer tip, there are a couple of preliminary steps you must take care of before you start squirting the glue. First, remove the caps from the tips of the cartridge. On urethane adhesives, it may be necessary to use a steel pin to remove a hardened chunk of material from the nozzle of the hardener side. Before applying the static mixer tip, balance the two sides of the cartridge by squirting material out onto a mixing board until both sides start to flow evenly. Each side of the cartridge kit is filled separately by the manufacturer, so the sides probably won't contain exactly the same amount of material. Balancing the cartridge will even out the quantity of material in each side.

Some static mixer tips allow you to adjust the amount of flow by trimming the size of the hole at the end. If you don't need a small bead, then trim it to the largest size, as this will make it easier and faster to squeeze the material out. Also, use the same size of mixer tip as comes packaged with the adhesive. Mixer tips come in different lengths. Shorter tips are okay for less viscous adhesives like urethanes as they mix more easily

than thicker adhesives. If you use a mixer tip that's too short for your adhesive, the components may not be properly mixed and may not cure out properly.

When everything is ready to go, attach the static mixer tip to the end of the cartridge. Make sure the repair area where you want to apply the adhesive is ready to go and that you've got whatever reinforcement or additional supplies you need during the application process. Once you start squirting the adhesive through the mixer tip, the clock starts ticking. If, during the process, you stop applying the adhesive, it will harden in the mixer tip, requiring you to replace the tip before continuing.

Before applying the adhesive to the part directly, squirt out a two- to three-inch ribbon of material on a mixing board to ensure that both sides are flowing evenly. If there is some blockage preventing one side from flowing, the mixture ratio will not be correct and the adhesive will not cure properly.

Once you're satisfied that both sides are flowing evenly and you're getting a uniform, consistent bead of material from the end of your mixer tip, immediately move the mixer tip over the repair area and apply a bead of adhesive down the middle of your repair area. Lay the gun down and spread the adhesive out using a plastic body spreader. While the adhesive is still "open" (i.e., wet, or uncured), you may insert reinforcing materials as necessary or apply an extra coating of adhesive. Don't wait too long, as the adhesive may cure inside the mixer tip. If that happens, you'll have to throw that tip away and get a new one.

While we're on this subject, it's important to choose an adhesive with an appropriate open or working time. If you want to apply adhesive over a large area, choose an adhesive with a working time that will allow you to apply a coat, insert reinforcing, and apply a finishing coat before it cures. This may take 10 to 15 minutes. If so, choose a slow-cure adhesive. If you're just applying the adhesive on a three-inch crack, then a standard five-minute cure adhesive will be a good choice. Some adhesives cure in as fast as 90 seconds, but this is far too fast to allow you any time to work with the adhesive in between

Cosmetic Repairs with Two-Part Repair Materials

Cosmetic repairs with two-part adhesives are commonly performed on minor surface damage, such as gouges, or when another repair technique, such as welding, is used to create the structural repair. Cosmetic repairs are not as demanding as structural repairs, but care must still be taken when preparing the surface to maximize the adhesion of the filler to the substrate. ■

1. Grind a shallow V-groove into the plastic in the damaged area with coarse sandpaper (50- to 80-grit). Use 80- to 180-grit paper on soft TPO substrates. Because the filler will serve only a cosmetic purpose, there is no need to go too wide or too deep with the V-groove. Simply grind the plastic flush to provide space for the filler to reside. Grind the plastic by hand or with a low-speed rotary sander; high-speed air powered sanders can create excessive friction heat that may actually melt the plastic.

2. Using a DA sander at low speed, sand inside the V-groove and round off the transition to the surrounding area with 80- to 180-grit sandpaper. Remove the paint in an area about 1/2 inch all around the V-groove, and scratch the paint for an area about one inch all around. The key is to create a smooth transition from painted surface to V-groove and back again. Blow the area dust-free with clean, dry compressed air.

3. If the substrate is a polyolefin, like TPO or PP, apply an adhesion promoter as recommended by the manufacturer of the two-part repair material you have selected. Apply the adhesion promoter and allow the solvents to flash off according to product instructions. Wait for the prescribed time before applying the repair material.

(cont. on next page)

Cosmetic Repairs with Two-Part Materials (Cont.)

4. Mix the adhesive according to product instructions. If packaged in individual squeeze tubes, dispense the appropriate amount on a mixing board and mix thoroughly until the color of the putty is uniform. If using a cartridge with a static mixer tip, dispense according to the directions. After mixing, immediately apply a smooth, even layer of repair material with a body spreader. Allow the filler to cure for the prescribed time before sanding. On TPO substrates, the longer you can wait, the better.

5. Rough contour and feather out the repair material with 80-grit in either a block sander or a DA. If working on a TPO, switch to 120- or 180-grit before you begin featheredging the material out onto the surface. Apply more filler over any low spots. Finish sand the area smooth with 180- or 220-grit before proceeding to the refinishing step.

squirts. If you use too fast an adhesive, you'll be tossing out lots of expensive mixer tips!

If you allow the adhesive to cure before you can insert the reinforcement or apply the second coat, you'll need to abrade the surface of the cured adhesive before you apply the second layer. The second layer of adhesive will not "melt into" the first layer, so you'll have to prepare again just like you're starting from scratch. That's why it's easier and often faster to choose an adhesive with a longer open time up front, especially when you're working on the backside and you want to apply reinforcement to the adhesive. With a longer open time, you'll have more time to insert your reinforcement and get the second layer on.

Finally, when you have finished applying the final layer of adhesive, you may choose to smooth the backside of the repair by laying down a sheet of clear polyethylene film. If you do this while the adhesive is still wet, you can smooth the repair material out and remove air bubbles by working them out by hand. Leave the film on the adhesive until it cures. When you peel the film up, you will have a smooth and hopefully bubble-free patch of repair material supporting your damage on the backside.

Prepare the Frontside of the Damage

Once the adhesive on the backside of the damage is cured, you can prepare the frontside for adhesive application. The "frontside" is the cosmetic side, or the side you'll want to sand smooth and refinish. To allow the repair material to remain on the surface after sanding, you have to V-groove or bevel into the damaged area. The larger the area over which you can spread the repair material, the stronger your repair will be. Therefore, a wide V-groove is better than a narrow one with regard to strength. Use your judgment, however. A small crack on an unstressed part won't need a two-inch-wide V-groove; probably a half-inch would be plenty. For structural repairs in critical areas, however, you'll probably want at least a two-inch-wide V-groove.

The fastest way to remove the plastic when creating a V-groove is with a carbide cutting burr in an air or electric die grinder. If you try to remove a lot of plastic with sandpaper alone, you risk running out of patience before the V-groove is properly prepared. If you ground the backside flat, you'll want your V-groove on the frontside to go all the way through the plastic. If you V-grooved the backside halfway through, you'll want to do the same on the front. The best way to determine if your frontside V-groove is deep enough is to V-groove down until the width of the crack starts to increase slightly. That way, you'll know you're getting into the V-groove on the other side.

After removing the plastic with the die grinder, scratch the inside of the V-groove with coarse sandpaper (36- to 80-grit). This will put a coarse sandscratch into the plastic, which is essential for good adhesion. After scratching the inside of the V-groove, radius or round off the edges of the V-groove out onto the surrounding area with 80-grit paper, preferably in a dual-action (DA) sander. If the part is painted on the frontside, remove at least 3/4 inch of the paint surrounding the V-groove with the 80-grit paper. Finally, using some 180-grit paper, scratch the paint for an area about one inch outside of the V-groove. By making a smooth transition from the V-groove out onto the surrounding area, you'll improve the quality of the featheredge you get when you finish sand the repair material.

A word of caution here. I generally recommended that you use 36- to 80-grit paper when preparing the V-groove. This puts some deep sandscratches into the plastic that will provide some mechanical locking when the adhesive is applied. One exception is on unpainted, textured TPO substrates. TPO is the material of choice on most late-model car bumper covers and many of them have a fine texture molded into the outer surface for cosmetic reasons. If you sand the area surrounding the V-groove with 80-grit or coarser sandpaper, the resulting sandscratches are almost impossible to hide during the refinish stage. Put some 80-grit scratches inside the V-groove, but when radiusing out onto the surface of the plastic, use nothing coarser than 180-grit sandpaper. A good rule of thumb on textured TPO plastics is to not sand with anything coarser than 180-grit on any surface that will have to be refinished.

When the V-groove is thoroughly scratched up and radiused out onto the surrounding area, blow the sanding dust off with clean, dry compressed air. If you choose to reapply a cleaning solution at this stage, make sure that all the solvents are completely evaporated by either allowing plenty of time or by lightly heating the area with a heat gun. Once the surface is dry and dust-free, you'll be ready to apply the adhesive.

If the plastic is TPO or some other olefin, apply an adhesion promoter as recommended by the manufacturer of the two-part repair material you are planning to use. Some two-parts don't require an adhesion promoter on TPO, but most do. Make sure you thoroughly read the manufacturer's instructions before proceeding with the application.

Apply Adhesive to the Frontside As I discussed previously in this chapter, depending on the type of adhesive you choose, you may either mix the two-part by hand or apply it using a cartridge gun and a static mixer tip. Either way, spread the adhesive using a plastic (polyethylene) body spreader over the V-groove to a level slightly higher than the part's surface. This will allow you to sand back the excess material to achieve the final profile without adding a second coat of adhesive.

Use of an epoxy adhesive, as opposed to a urethane adhesive, on the frontside of the repair will help to ease sanding of the repair material. Some autobody technicians will use a urethane two-part on the backside for strength and an epoxy on the frontside for easy sandability. The choice depends on your expectations for the strength of the finished repair. If strength trumps ease of sanding, then use a urethane two-part on both sides. On rigid substrates like SMC, the strength and toughness advantage of a urethane is not as great as it is on more flexible substrates. On SMC, epoxies can be just as strong as urethanes since flexibility isn't a factor.

According to the directions provided by the manufacturer of the two-part material, allow sufficient time for the adhesive to cure before sanding it. A good rule of thumb is to allow as much time as possible. If you can wait overnight, do so. Most fast-cure materials claim that they are

Structural Repairs on SMC with Cyanoacrylate Adhesives

The long glass fibers and mineral fillers in SMC soak up liquid like crazy. Use this effect to your advantage by using a thin CA adhesive to bond the material back together. The CA will wick into the substrate by capillary action and form a strong, rigid bond in seconds. ■

1. Spray CA accelerator into the frayed ends of the broken SMC. This will place the alkaline initiating chemical throughout the depth of the crack, allowing the CA to cure from within.

2. Fit the cracked pieces of SMC back together as closely as possible. Intertwine the frayed glass fibers to the maximum extent possible. SMC distorts when damaged, so it will be hard to do this perfectly, but get it as close as you can. Tape or clamp the parts together to hold them in place until you can apply the adhesive.

3. Soak the damaged area with a water-thin CA adhesive. The adhesive will be drawn into the crack by capillary action and form strong bonds between the glass fibers. Spray more accelerator to quick cure any excess CA glue.

4. To create the best structural repair, rough grind the backside and apply a coating of a rigid, SMC repair material with embedded glass fiber reinforcement. Finish the cosmetic appearance by grinding the frontside slightly flush and applying a skim coat of the SMC repair material.

sandable in as little as 20 to 30 minutes. At this point, the two-part may have only achieved a 70 percent cure; it's cured enough to allow it to be sanded, but it hasn't reached its full strength.

If you're working with a rigid plastic, like SMC or PC, you'll have no problems if you sand it at this stage. However, if you have a TPO substrate, you'll definitely get better adhesion and a better featheredge if you wait until a full cure is achieved. At a room temperature of 75 degrees, it may take 12 to 24 hours for the adhesive to fully cure. Heating the area with a heat lamp will accelerate this process. By heating the material, the molecules will be able to move more freely and complete the crosslinking reaction more quickly. If you choose to accelerate the cure with a heat lamp, be careful not to overheat the substrate. Hold the lamp back from the surface sufficiently to achieve a surface temperature of approximately 140 degrees F. At this temperature, a full cure of the adhesive will be achieved in one to two hours. Allow the material to cool completely before sanding.

Finish Sanding the Frontside   On the cosmetic side of your repair, one of your main goals is to have your repair be invisible after the part is refinished. The only way to achieve this is to create the smoothest possible transition from the surface of the repair material to the surface of the substrate. This involves sanding the entire area either laboriously by hand or more quickly with a power sander. The best way to go about this depends on the type of plastic you're working with.

If you're working with a rigid plastic, like SMC, PC, fiberglass, or ABS, you can start the sanding process with a heavier grit sandpaper. In general, there are two risks you take using a coarse (36- to 50-grit) sandpaper during the finish sanding process. First, you risk creating deep sandscratches that will be difficult or impossible to remove later on in the sanding process. Second, a heavier grit sandpaper is more likely to cause the repair material to peel up at the featheredge during the sanding process.

These two risks are not as much a problem on rigid plastics as they are on flexible ones, especially on TPO. For one thing, if the substrate is rigid, you're likely to be able to use an easy-

sanding polyester glaze as a finish filler, enabling you to fill any heavy sandscratches you created during the initial roughing-in process. Two-part repair materials, especially those for use on rigid plastics, are formulated first for strength and second for sandability. Epoxy two-parts, which are usually easier to sand than urethane two-parts, are still more difficult to sand than are polyester fillers. Therefore, on rigid plastics, it is usually faster to rough-in the epoxy filler and give it a second glaze coat of polyester body filler to finish. This is especially true when your repair area is fairly large and you're likely to have to apply two or three coats of repair material to fill in all the low spots and imperfections. On smaller repair areas, you may be able to complete the sanding process with only the initial coat of repair material, so you probably won't need to use a polyester glaze. In such a case, it would be better to sand with nothing coarser than 80-grit to prevent creating deep sandscratches. The only thing you need to watch out for here is that some urethane two-part adhesives are not compatible with subsequent polyester glaze coats. Check the manufacturer's directions before attempting to use a polyester glaze. You're usually safe with an epoxy two-part, however.

The second reason that you can safely use coarse sandpaper on rigid substrates is that two-part materials generally don't have a problem with adhesion on rigid plastics, so a coarse sandpaper is not likely to peel up the repair material at the featheredge as long as the surface preparation was done properly.

Although laborious, the way to get the best appearance at the end of the finish sanding process is to do your initial sanding by hand with either a block sander or, preferably, a long fileboard sander. Using the coarsest sandpaper you feel safe with (40-grit is about the coarsest you'll want to go, even on rigid substrates), sand the area in an X-pattern over the repair material. If you've crowned the repair material over the V-groove, it'll probably take you a few minutes of effort to get the surface close to flush with the surrounding area. Again, if you're working on a rigid plastic and you're planning to use a polyester skim coat, keep sanding with the heavy grit paper until you've completely smoothed and feathered the repair material out onto the surface. If you're working on a softer substrate or don't plan to use a polyester skim coat, switch to a finer grit of paper (80-, 120-, or 180-grit) just before you start to feather the repair material out onto the surface.

Roughing-in the profile of the repair material correctly is the key to getting an invisible repair at the end. Too often, in haste, people will rough-in the filler using power tools like a DA sander or, worse yet, a rotary grinder. These tools do not spread the sanding forces out over a large enough area and are, thus, likely to cause dips or waves in the filler. They may be hard to detect by hand, but if the part is to be painted and clearcoated, they will become very obvious at that point. Even air-powered fileboards should be used with caution as they remove material very quickly and can magnify any mistakes you make. Working by hand takes longer, but it enables you to very easily check the progress as you go along. Taking a little more time up front with the first step of the sanding process will save you a lot of time later correcting mistakes.

If you're working on a TPO substrate, stay away from anything coarser than 80-grit to avoid gouging the soft plastic too deeply (except on textured, unpainted TPO substrates, where you don't want to touch the plastic with anything coarser than 180-grit). If the surface was prepared properly before the two-part was applied and as long as the two-part is sufficiently cured, the repair material shouldn't peel up at the featheredge using 80-grit paper. Rough-in the profile using 80-grit in a block by hand, then switch to 120- or 180-grit once you get almost finished to obtain the final profile and featheredge.

Once you're satisfied with the roughed-in profile, you can continue sanding with finer grits. If you started with a 40-grit fileboard, move to an 80-grit. It's still preferable to use a block at this stage, but once you've got the proper profile roughed in, using a DA at this stage won't be a problem either. If you are planning to use a polyester glaze, do so after sanding with the 80-grit.

When applying second coats of repair material or polyester glazes, make sure you have sandscratched the entire surface over which you plan to apply the filler. After roughing-in the first coat, you'll often have low spots that the sandpaper didn't touch. These low spots are likely to be smooth and shiny. If you apply a second coat of filler over these smooth and shiny spots, the filler won't stick. Remember, two-part repair materials are thermosetting, or crosslinking, plastics, so the second layer isn't going to "melt in" to the first coat. Before you apply the second coat of filler, remove the shine from these low spots by sanding with 80-grit by hand.

When sanding the second coat of filler, don't use anything coarser than 80-grit sandpaper (assuming that you're getting close to the finished profile). Again, block-sanding is preferable, especially when your second coat has covered most of the first coat, but a DA may be used if you just had to fill in a few spots here and there. If you still have low spots after the sanding the second coat, repeat the process for a third coat.

You may notice some pinholes in the surface of the repair material. These are air bubbles that were entrapped in the repair material during the application process. They are difficult to fill because the surfaces inside the pinholes are smooth and glossy. When you try to spread a filler into them, it seems that the filler comes right back out again when you move the body spreader over them. As long as the pinholes are small, it is best to fill them up with a spot putty after applying the first coat of primer surfacer. If the pinhole is larger than 1/16 inch or 2mm, it's better to sand it out and refill it with repair material before you prime the part.

Once you've filled all the low spots, smooth everything out with 180- or 220-grit sandpaper. These grits are fine enough for a primer surfacer to fill any scratches that might be created in the surface. The next step in the repair process will be to refinish the surface, which I'll begin covering in Chapter 5.

Cosmetic Repairs with Two-Part Adhesives/Fillers

The most common use of two-part repair materials is as a cosmetic filler. If the damage is just a

Structural Repairs on Rigid Plastics with Cyanoacrylate Adhesives

Cyanoacrylate adhesives stick well to rigid plastics, like ABS and PC, but because of the brittle nature of CA adhesives, they can't provide a good structural repair that will resist tensile and bending loads unless reinforced with a patch that laps over the joint on at least one, and preferably both, sides. ■

Tacking Together Tight-Fitting Cracks

1. Apply CA accelerator to both cracked surfaces. This allows the CA to cure from within the crack.

2. Tape or clamp the broken pieces tightly together.

3. Apply water-thin CA to the crack. The adhesive will wick into the crack via capillary action and will cure from within. Spray more accelerator to quick-cure any excess adhesive.

Tacking Together Cracks with Gaps

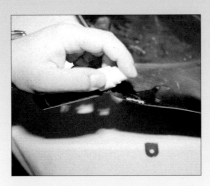  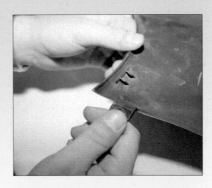

1. Apply CA accelerator to only one surface.

2. Apply thicker, gap-filling CA or CA gel to the other surface.

3. Fit parts together tightly. Clamp or tape pieces together until glue cures sufficiently to allow handling. Spray more accelerator to quick-cure any excess adhesive.

(cont. on next page)

Structural Repairs on Rigid Plastics with Cyanoacrylate Adhesives (Cont.)

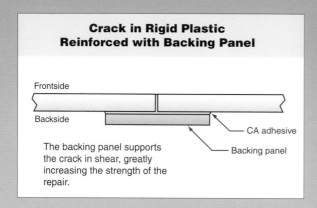

Crack in Rigid Plastic Reinforced with Backing Panel

Frontside

Backside

CA adhesive

Backing panel

The backing panel supports the crack in shear, greatly increasing the strength of the repair.

Reinforcing a Crack with a Plastic Backing Panel

1. Cut a backing panel from a scrap piece of the same type of plastic. The piece must fit tightly against the surface of the damaged part along the entire length of the crack to be effective. If the backing panel does not fit tightly or if the damaged part has complex contours, use a rigid two-part adhesive to make a backing patch. Remove any paint from the backing panel and sand the surface to be bonded with 180-grit sandpaper.

2. Remove any paint and sand the cracked area flush with 180-grit paper. Sand an area large enough to extend beyond the edges of the backing panel when it is in place. Blow dust-free with compressed air.

3. Apply CA accelerator to the side of the backing panel to be bonded. Allow the solvent to evaporate.

4. Orient the damaged panel so the crack is facing up if possible. Apply water-thin CA over the area where the backing patch will be applied.

5. Immediately after applying CA adhesive to damaged panel, press the backing panel into place. Keep firm pressure on the panel until the adhesive has cured to handling strength. Finish the repair by filling crack on the frontside with rigid two-part filler.

Reinforcing a Crack with a Two-Part Adhesive Backing Patch

1. Rough grind the plastic on the backside of the damaged area with 50- to 80-grit sandpaper in a low-speed rotary grinder. Remove any paint and grind an area two to three inches wide all along the crack. Make sure you scratch the surface anywhere you plan to apply adhesive. Blow dust-free with compressed air.

2. Mix a rigid two-part filler and apply in a two- to three-inch-wide swath over the crack on the backside. Embed reinforcing material if desired. ■

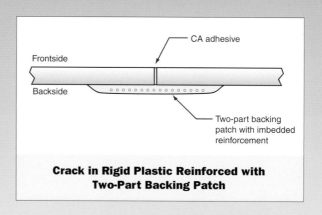

CA adhesive

Frontside

Backside

Two-part backing patch with imbedded reinforcement

Crack in Rigid Plastic Reinforced with Two-Part Backing Patch

gouge or dent—i.e., where the structural integrity of the part is not compromised—a two-part filler is ideal for leveling the surface out in preparation for refinishing. Cosmetic fillers are also necessary when other methods such as welding or cyanoacrylate adhesives are used to make the structural repair. When used in such an application, the strength of the filler is not as important as its compatibility with the substrate and its sandability.

If the part is rigid, you may use any variety of rigid two-parts or polyester filler. Epoxy two-parts are normally chosen over urethanes for their easy sandability. Polyester fillers are even easier to sand, but are not as strong as epoxy. Since strength is not the main priority for a cosmetic fill, polyester filler can be chosen in most instances.

If the part is even a little bit flexible, stay away from polyester fillers. They are too rigid for flexible applications. They will pop off or crack if the part is flexed. This is one of the most common and easily avoidable errors committed by bodyshop technicians when repairing bumper covers. Fortunately, there are a wide variety of epoxy, urethane, or acrylic two-part systems available on the market for doing flexible repairs. Since epoxies and acrylic two-parts are easier to sand than urethanes, they are usually chosen for cosmetic repairs.

For surface preparation and application of a cosmetic filler, the same process is followed as for the frontside of a structural repair with two-part adhesives. Since I covered this in the previous section, I won't go into great detail here, but I will summarize the main steps in performing a cosmetic fill.

Assuming that the plastic has already been cleaned, the first step is to prepare the surface by V-grooving with sandpaper. For a cosmetic fill, it is not necessary to take the V-groove all the way through the plastic, or even halfway. All you need to do is sand the surface slightly flush to provide space for the filler. As a result, you don't need to use a die grinder to remove the plastic as a coarse sandpaper will usually be sufficient to grind in a shallow V-groove.

For all plastics other than TPO, use a 50- to 80-grit grinding disc to create the V-groove.

Since TPOs are soft, 80-grit is as coarse as you want to go, and even this is too coarse for unpainted, textured TPOs. When doing repairs on such plastics, don't sand outside the V-groove with anything coarser than 180-grit.

It is always preferable to use a low-speed electric tool as opposed to an air-powered tool when grinding the V-groove. If the grinding is done too fast, the friction heat generated by the sandpaper could melt or smear the substrate, especially on TPOs. Electric tools have high torque at low speeds, allowing you to put your sandscratches into the surface without risking melting or smearing the plastic during the process. Air tools have low torque at low speeds, and only work well when they are spinning very fast, so there is a definite risk of melting the plastic, especially on TPOs.

During the V-grooving process, smooth out any sharp or ragged edges. You'll want to achieve a V-groove that's shaped more like a U-groove with rounded or radiused edges all the way around. Sand inside the V-groove with coarse sandpaper, and then remove the paint in the area surrounding the V-groove (for about 1/2 inch) with 80-grit paper (180-grit for textured, unpainted TPO). For an area about one inch outside of this area, scratch the paint with 180-grit paper. When you're finished preparing the surface, there should be a smooth transition from flat to V-groove and back again.

Once the V-groove has been prepared, remove the sanding dust using clean, dry compressed air or a clean cloth. Remove all the dust from the little nooks and crannies you've created in the surface with the sandpaper. If you choose to apply a cleaning solvent after removing the dust, give the solvent plenty of time to evaporate, or preferably, use a heat gun to heat the area lightly.

The last step before you apply the filler is to use an adhesion promoter if necessary. This step is usually only necessary on PP or TPO substrates. Refer to the instructions provided by the manufacturer of the two-part material you've chosen to use.

Mix the two-part repair material according to the manufacturer's directions. Many times when you're applying a cosmetic fill over a small area, it is more economical and faster to use an epoxy system that can be squeezed out and mixed by hand as opposed to a cartridge gun with a static mixer tip. The mixer tips themselves usually cost at least $1.00, not to mention the cost of the material wasted inside the mixer tip. Cartridge application systems are more appropriate for larger repair areas.

Using a plastic body spreader, smooth the repair material over the V-groove and crown it slightly to allow for sanding later. You'll want the edges of the filler to extend slightly out onto the area where you've scratched the paint, but not beyond that.

Allow the filler plenty of time to cure. Although most fast-cure fillers are sandable after 30 minutes or so, they have usually not achieved a 100-percent cure in that amount of time. This is usually not a problem on rigid plastics and urethane, but a full cure is preferred if the substrate is TPO. Either allow the filler to cure overnight, or accelerate the cure with a heat lamp. Allowing the filler to reach its full strength will give you a better featheredge when the filler is sanded.

To achieve the optimum finished appearance, I recommend first sanding the repair material by hand with a block sander or fileboard block. If you are repairing a rigid plastic, you can start with 40-grit paper and switch to 80-grit as you approach the final profile. On TPO, start with 80-grit and switch to 120 or 180 as you get close to the finished profile. Roughing-in the shape of the filler properly at first is the key to getting a perfect finished repair.

After rough sanding the filler, fill in any low spots as necessary with a second coat. Remember to rough up any smooth and shiny areas in your low spots before you apply the second coat. On rigid plastics, a polyester glaze coat is a good choice for a final filler as long as the underlying two-part repair material is compatible with it. Again, don't use polyester fillers on flexible or semi-flexible plastics.

Once you've removed all the low spots and you're satisfied with the rough profile of the repair area, finish sand with 180- or 220-grit sandpaper. This will provide a surface to which the primer surfacer coat will stick well and leave sandscratches small enough for the primer surfacer to fill effectively. The next step would be to refinish the surface, a topic that is covered in Chapter 5.

Repair with Cyanoacrylate Adhesives

Cyanoacrylate is the tongue-twisting technical term for a family of adhesives that are popularly known as Super Glues or Krazy Glues. These are both trademarks used by different manufacturers, so I'll just call them cyanoacrylates or CAs for short.

Cyanoacrylates are single-part, solvent-free adhesives that form strong bonds on a variety of substrates, including many plastics. The crosslinking reaction in the cyanoacrylate resin is initiated by moisture adsorbed from the air or by the use of accelerator chemicals containing an alkaline material.

There are three types of CA adhesives—ethyl/methyl, allyl, and alkoxy alkyl—but the one most commonly used in consumer applications is ethyl/methyl because of its relatively long shelf life and superior bonding strength. This is the type of CA I'll be referring to in this book.

There are several advantages to CA adhesives:

- CAs are very easy to apply. They don't require mixing, clamping, or heat to cure.

- With proper joint design, CAs create bonds with high strength on a variety of materials including metals, ceramics, elastomers, and most plastics (excluding polyolefins like PP, PE, and TPO).

- CAs are very fast, curing to handling strength within seconds and achieving full cure in a matter of minutes.

- CAs are economical to use. In a properly designed joint, a small amount of adhesive will spread over a large area. The strength of a CA bond depends on surface-to-surface contact between the substrates to be joined, so the bond line is very thin. For this reason, very little CA is needed to create a strong bond.

Some of CAs disadvantages are:

Cosmetic Repairs with Cyanoacrylate Adhesive and Filler Powder

Gouges and holes in rigid, non-olefin plastics can be quickly and easily filled with a combination of filler powder and water-thin CA adhesive. In this sequence, I'll assume you have a hole you need to fill. Filling a gouge is similar except you wouldn't need to use any backing tape. ■

1. Sand a bevel around the edges of the hole or gouge with 80-grit sandpaper. Sandscratch the surrounding area to maximize adhesion and featheredge of the CA glue. Blow dust-free with compressed air.

2. Apply aluminum-backed body tape to the opposite side of the hole to prevent filler powder and glue from falling through.

3. Spray CA accelerator inside the hole and in the surrounding area. Allow the solvents to flash off.

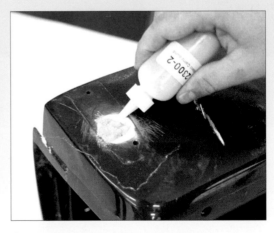

4. Sprinkle filler powder into the hole.

(cont. on next page)

Cosmetic Repairs with CA and Filler Powder (Cont.)

5. Smooth out filler powder with a body spreader or popsicle stick.

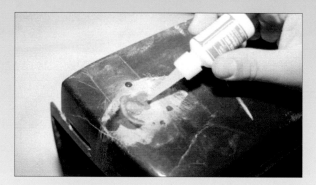

6. Soak the powder with water-thin CA adhesive. The CA should cure from within due to accelerator within the powder. The adhesive should cure in 10 to 20 seconds.

7. After the adhesive hardens, sand with 80- or 120-grit sandpaper. Fill any remaining porosity with more powder and CA glue, or apply a skim coat of rigid two-part filler material.

- CAs are brittle when cured and thus have low impact and peel strength.
- The strength of a CA bond is largely dependent on the design of the joint. CAs can be very strong when loaded in shear, but will likely fail if loaded in tension or bending. In most repair situations, your freedom to design a proper joint to take advantage of CA's strengths is constrained. Usually you're faced with a tear in the part, resulting in a butt joint that will be subjected mainly to tensile and bending loads as opposed to shear loads.
- CAs can be hazardous to the user. They cure quickly in the presence of moisture and, thus, will bond your skin together in seconds. Most CAs have low viscosity and are likely to run off into areas where you don't want them to be, like on your fingers.

In the realm of plastic repair, CAs are useful for doing structural repairs only on very rigid plastics with relatively high surface energies like SMC, ABS, and PC. They are also useful for tacking broken pieces together while you perform a repair using a different method.

CAs won't stick to low-surface-energy polyolefins like PP, PE, and TPO. Also, due to the brittle nature of CAs, they won't hold up on substrates that are semi-flexible, like nylon motorcycle fairings. Despite these limitations, CAs are a very useful tool to keep in the toolbox.

Structural Repairs with Cyanoacrylate Adhesives

Good structural repairs can be performed with CA adhesives if the plastic is very rigid and if there is sufficient surface area over which the adhesive can be spread. It is especially strong on SMC if the long glass fibers can be woven together prior to application of the adhesive. However, if you have a clean break in a PC or ABS substrate, a CA adhesive will not provide a good structural repair unless you reinforce the broken area.

Structural Repairs on SMC Surface preparation for cracks in SMC differs from that for any other plastic. There is glass fiber and talc exposed at the raw edge of a broken SMC panel. If water or a cleaning solvent is applied, the exposed talc and glass fiber will soak it right into the panel, possibly damaging the structure of the material. For this reason, it is not usually recommended that you repair an SMC panel that has been exposed to the elements for any length of time after the damage occurs.

We use this tendency for the fibers and talc to soak up liquid to our advantage when using CA adhesives. Without first cleaning the plastic, fit the broken edges together as closely as possible, allowing the fibers to intertwine. This is sometimes difficult to do, because the fibers may resist intertwining if there is further deformation in the area. The key is to fit them as closely and tightly together as possible. This creates a very large surface area over which the adhesive will be applied.

Once the panels are in their proper positions, soak the broken area with a thin cyanoacrylate adhesive (of water-like consistency). The thin adhesive will wick into all the nooks and crannies between the fibers, creating a very strong repair. Such a repair can be further reinforced with a patch of rigid two-part material on the backside. The same two-part compound can be used to finish out the cosmetic appearance on the frontside. Simply grind a shallow V-groove along the crack on the frontside and fill with rigid two-part. Such a repair, with cyanoacrylate in the core and epoxy on both sides, will be extremely strong and durable.

Structural Repairs on ABS/PC

A different approach has to be taken with these rigid thermoplastics since they don't have the long strands of glass fibers into which the CA can soak into and adhere. If the damage is a clean break and the crack can be fitted together tightly (i.e., a butt joint), a CA will bond ABS and PC together very well. However, if the repair is subjected to any load, particularly tensile or bending load, the repair will likely fail. Butt joint repairs must be reinforced with a lap joint in order for a CA repair to be considered structural.

Because of this requirement for reinforcement, and the fact that there are easier ways to repair ABS and PC (for reasons we'll discover in a moment), the repair technician will often choose to use plastic welding or a two-part adhesive (or both simultaneously) to create a structural repair. However, cyanoacrylates will often be used to tack the broken pieces back together while a repair is being done by another method.

But good structural repairs can be made with CAs. The key is to use a tight-fitting backing plate of the same material to lap over the cracked area and support it in shear. It is actually best to fit a backing plate on both sides of the joint, as shown in the accompanying sidebar, but this is usually not possible due to cosmetic considerations.

In contrast with SMC, you'll want to clean the plastic with soap and water and with a plastic cleaning solvent before applying the adhesive.

Before you tack a tight-fitting crack back together with CA, first spray the activator or accelerator on both cracked surfaces and allow the solvents to evaporate. This will deposit an alkaline chemical onto the surface of the crack, which will cause the CA to cure more quickly.

Fit the broken pieces together and hold them with aluminum-backed tape, clamps, or by some other means. Don't depend on your hands to hold the pieces steady enough during the curing process. Once all the cracks are clamped tightly together, apply a thin CA (with water-like viscosity) along the crack. The CA will be wicked through the crack by capillary action, just as it is with SMC. The CA should cure to handling strength in just 10 to 15 seconds, allowing you to continue with the repair process immediately.

In contrast with the surface preparation used for two-part adhesives, when using CA adhesives, it is not desirable to put a heavy sandscratch in the surface between the reinforcing patch and the panel. With CA adhesive repairs, thin bond lines yield the best strength, so a heavy sandscratching of the plastic will actually separate the reinforcing patch and panel. After cleaning the panels, it is good to sand lightly with a fine sandpaper (320- to 400-grit) just to remove the shine from the surfaces.

Ideally, the reinforcing patch should be made of the same material and should match the profile of the panel to be repaired. Furthermore, the reinforcing patch should be pressed into close

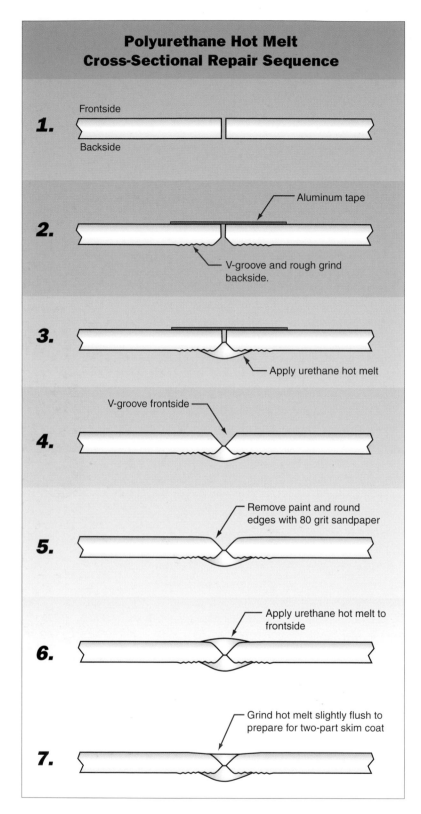

Polyurethane Hot Melt Cross-Sectional Repair Sequence

1. Frontside / Backside

2. Aluminum tape — V-groove and rough grind backside.

3. Apply urethane hot melt

4. V-groove frontside

5. Remove paint and round edges with 80 grit sandpaper

6. Apply urethane hot melt to frontside

7. Grind hot melt slightly flush to prepare for two-part skim coat

contact with the panel to be repaired, all along the length of the crack. In practice, due to the complex curves and shapes of most plastic parts on cars and motorcycles, this is difficult or impossible to do, which is why other repair techniques are more common on ABS and PC.

But, if you have a flat panel, this method will work well. Prior to clamping the reinforcing patch into place, spray one of the surfaces to be joined with the accelerator and allow the solvents to flash off. In this case, don't apply the accelerator to both panels. You'll want to put drops of glue directly onto the panel without the accelerator (preferably the one that's oriented *up*, so the glue doesn't run off before you apply your patch). Apply a water-thin CA; use about a drop to cover each square inch to be covered by your reinforcing patch.

Once you've got the glue down and the reinforcing patch ready to go, carefully align the part then quickly press them together. If you've done everything properly, the patch will be stuck instantly, which is why aligning the patch before you press it down is so important in the first place.

If you're not concerned about the cosmetic appearance of your repair, you can reinforce the opposite side of the damage in the same way, which will vastly increase the strength of the repair. As you can see, done properly, a CA can create a strong, permanent repair on ABS and PC substrates.

Cosmetic Repairs on Rigid Plastics with Cyanoacrylate Adhesives
Because of their speed, cyanoacrylate adhesives are attractive to those who need to finish their repairs very quickly, such as mobile technicians who do repairs on the spot in used car lots. Although not suitable for structural repairs, CAs used in combination with a filler powder can create very quick and easy repairs on gouges and holes in rigid plastics. If you are not in a big hurry to finish your repair, a two-part rigid filler/adhesive might be a better choice than a CA as you're more likely to get a smooth, paintable surface the first time with a two-part. But if speed is what you need, you can't beat a CA.

Repairing Cracks in Thermoset Urethane Substrates with Hot-Melt Urethane Welding Rod

Although this process is commonly called *welding,* thermoset urethanes cannot truly be fusion welded because the substrate is not meltable. Welding urethane refers to a process whereby thermoset urethane filler rod is melted and applied to the surface like a hot-melt glue. In this sense, it works like a brazing process since the base material is not melted. Done properly, a urethane hot-melt repair can be very strong, sometimes stronger than the substrate itself. ■

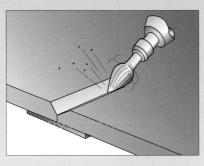

1. Grind a V-groove halfway through the backside of the part with a pointed die grinder cutting bit. Sand the V-groove with coarse sandpaper (80-grit or coarser) to put some extra "tooth" in the surface. Also, remove the paint in the area immediately surrounding the V-groove and round off the edges leading into the V-groove for extra strength. Blow the area dust-free with compressed air.

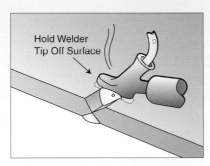

Hold Welder Tip Off Surface

2. With the airless plastic welder's temperature dial properly adjusted, feed thermoplastic urethane welding rod through the welder tip. The rod should come out the bottom of the completely melted and clear, not discolored, smoking, or bubbling. Holding the welder's tip slightly off the surface of the plastic, melt the rod into the V-groove. Slowly feed the rod into the welder's tip as you make your pass. Lay down no more than two inches of rod at a time. Remove the rod from the welder tip, and before the melted rod has time to cool down, go back over

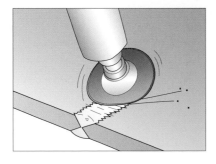

Hold Welder Tip Off Surface

3. After the weld cools, repeat the process of V-grooving and welding on the opposite side.

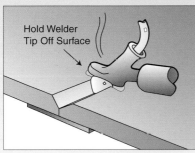

4. Using coarse sandpaper, grind the weld on the frontside slightly flush so it may be covered with a flexible two-part filler.

Repairing Torn Bolt Holes in Thermoset Urethane Substrates

Torn-out mounting holes are a very common occurrence on damaged urethane bumper covers. This sidebar shows how durable repairs can be easily done with the airless plastic welder and thermoplastic urethane filler rod. ■

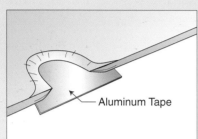

1. Taper the plastic all around the hole down to a point on both sides using a coarse sandpaper disc in a rotary grinder. Round off the edges and remove the paint for about 1/4 inch all around. Any area that will be covered with urethane welding rod should be sandscratched. Blow dust-free with compressed air.

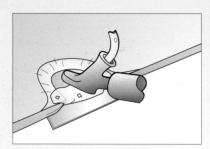

Aluminum Tape

2. Use aluminum-backed tape to create a bridge across the torn mounting hole. This will support the molten welding rod until it cools enough to harden.

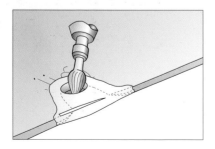

3. Melt thermoplastic urethane welding rod into the area, first around the edges of the taper, then continue toward the center. Smooth the filler rod out onto the substrate with welder tip, taking care not to overheat the base material. Fill the entire area, even the bolt hole. The hole will be drilled out later. Allow the filler rod to cool completely before going to next step.

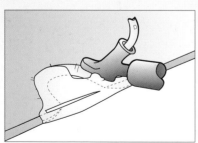

4. Working on the opposite side, peel off the tape. Melt some of the filler rod around the edge and smear it onto the tapered area to lock the existing block of filler material onto both sides. Then fill the remaining void around the taper with more urethane filler rod, taking care to melt the newly-added welding rod together with the existing block of material applied from the other side. Fill the area until it is flush with or slightly crowned over the surface. Allow to cool.

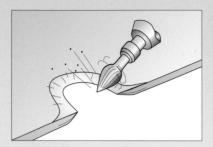

5. Drill the hole out with a twist drill bit, then open up the hole to the original dimensions with an die grinder. If you want to finish the repair cosmetically, sand the filler rod flush with the surface, then apply a skim coat of flexible two-part repair material.

First of all, the repair process is much easier if you can remove the damaged part so that it may be oriented horizontally during the repair process. Also, cyanoacrylates work well on small to medium gouges and holes. If the area gets too large, it's better to use a rigid two-part filler. After cleaning the plastic in the damaged area, sand a slight V-groove into the plastic with 80-grit sandpaper, taking care to round off the edges.

If you're going to fill a hole, apply some tape to the backside of the hole to keep the loose powder in place while you apply the adhesive. Blow the repair area dust-free, and you're ready to apply the adhesive.

Not all CA repair kits are packaged with filler powder. Make sure you select one that is if you want to do this kind of repair. Once you've got the proper materials in hand and are ready to go, spray a light coating of accelerator onto the surface and allow the solvents to flash off. Then sprinkle the filler powder into the gouge and smooth it evenly into the damaged area with a spatula or a popsicle stick. Finally, soak the powder completely with a low viscosity, water-thin CA adhesive. Most filler powders contain alkaline materials to catalyze the adhesive, but you may also spray on accelerator to speed the cure or to cure any excess adhesive in the surrounding area. CAs create heat when they cure, so much so that you may actually see vapor rise from the surface.

Once the adhesive is cured, it can be sanded immediately. Starting with 80- or 120-grit paper, sand the powder and any excess material in the area smooth. You may notice some porosity in the surface after sanding. This is due to the bubbling that occurs when the CA cures quickly in the presence of a lot of catalyst. Repeat the process or use a skim coat of two-part filler to fill these imperfections.

Using this method, filling gouges and holes in rigid plastic can be done in literally a matter of minutes. There is no other method that is quite as fast as cyanoacrylates. As long as the plastic is rigid and non-olefinic, then this method will be as durable as a two-part repair.

Repair with Hot-Melt Adhesives

Just as there are thermoplastic and thermoset *plastics,* there are also thermoplastic and thermoset *adhesives.* This makes sense, as all adhesives are plastics anyway. Most adhesives are thermoset—they are applied at room temperature in a liquid state, and through some irreversible chemical reaction with a catalyst, they eventually form a crosslinked solid material that cannot again be returned to a liquid state.

Thermoplastic adhesives are also widely used, mostly in industrial (especially packaging)

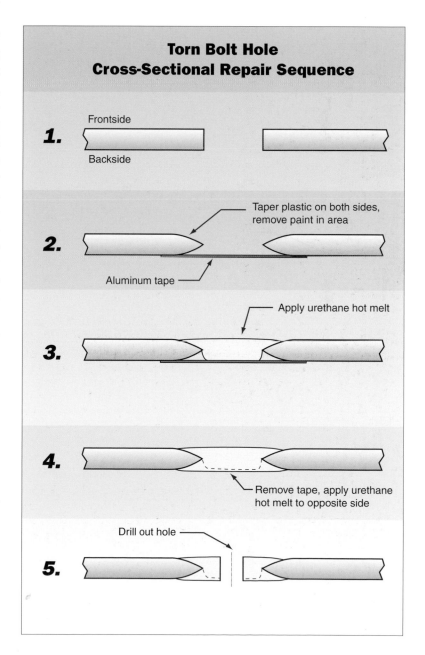

**Torn Bolt Hole
Cross-Sectional Repair Sequence**

1. Frontside / Backside

2. Taper plastic on both sides, remove paint in area / Aluminum tape

3. Apply urethane hot melt

4. Remove tape, apply urethane hot melt to opposite side

5. Drill out hole

applications, but there are also uses for them in the field of repair. Thermoplastic, or hot-melt, adhesives are heated to a liquid state, applied, and then allowed to cool back to a solid. Because they are not crosslinked, they may be reheated and melted again.

Because there is no crosslinking chemical reaction that needs to take place, thermoplastic adhesives are faster than thermoset ones. This is an advantage when a repair needs to be completed quickly. However, because thermoplastic repair adhesives do not form crosslinks, they are generally not as strong as thermoset adhesives.

There are two types of hot-melts used for plastic repair. One, thermoplastic urethane, is designed specifically for repairing thermoset urethane parts. The other, often called universal plastic welding rod, is an olefin-based material formulated with filler material to modify its properties for repair use.

Because hot-melt repair materials are usually applied using plastic welding equipment, there is some confusion in the trade regarding the application of these materials. Technicians without much experience with plastic welding often make the mistake of attempting to melt the substrate when applying the hot-melt material. The proper way to apply a hot-melt material is to melt it onto the surface, but not together with it. In separating this section on hot-melt adhesives from the section on plastic welding, I am attempting to reduce this confusion. Hopefully, by the end of this chapter, you will see hot-melt repair materials as being distinct from regular fusion welding filler rods.

Repairing Thermoset Urethane Substrates with Hot-Melt Urethane Welding Rod

Polyurethane is the only type of thermoset plastic that can be repaired with a plastic welder. It may seem strange to consider repairing thermosets with heat when thermosets are not meltable. However, when repairing thermoset urethanes with a plastic welder, you are *not* using the heat to melt the base material. You are simply using the heat of the welder to melt and apply a thermoplastic urethane hot-melt adhesive.

Hot-air welders are very difficult to use for the repair of thermoset urethane, because it is nearly impossible to keep from overheating the substrate during the welding process. It was this problem that led to the development of the airless plastic welder in the early 1980s by Jim Sparks, founder of Urethane Supply Company. Using the airless plastic welder, the thermoplastic urethane filler rod can be melted and spread

Polyurethane Hot Melt Cross-Sectional Repair Sequence

1. Vinyl Skin
   Urethane Foam

2. V-groove crack and taper out vinyl skin

3. Apply urethane hot melt

4. Grind hot melt slightly flush, feather back surrounding area

5. Apply skim coat of two-part filler

6. Sand filler flush

Repairing Tears in Padded Dashboards

As of this writing, dashboards are just beginning to make a transition to TPO skin over TPO foam. However, the vast majority of dashboards are still PVC skin over urethane foam. Cracks and tears in the PVC skin can be repaired as long as the skin still has some pliability. However, if the dash is sun-damaged to the point where it is brittle all over, it's probably not worth repairing. ■

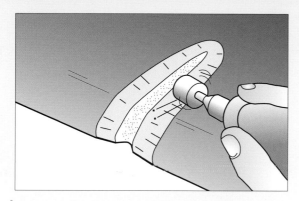

1. After cleaning the dash pad, open up the crack slightly with an electric die grinder tool. The crack has to be open to allow the urethane welding rod to get underneath the skin and interlock with the underlying urethane foam. Open up a cavity at least 1/4-inch deep in the foam backing and vinyl cover. Sand and bevel the edges of the vinyl cover around the cavity to allow for featheredging of the filler. Round off the edges of the V-groove and create a smooth transition to the surrounding area.

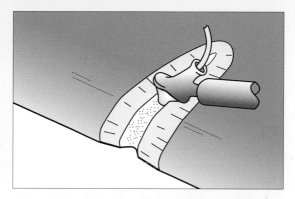

2. Melt thermoplastic urethane welding rod into the bottom of the cavity with an airless plastic welder. Hold the welding tip slightly off the surface and use it to deposit melted welding rod into the V-groove. After filling about one inch of the V-groove, remove the welding rod from the welder and use the welder tip to press the urethane rod into the foam and smooth it out over the vinyl skin.

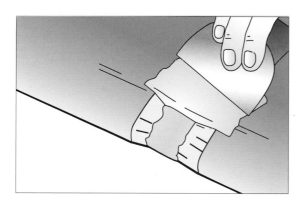

3. After allowing the weld area to cool, grind the urethane rod flush with the surface using coarse sandpaper. Mix a flexiblized polyester or two-part epoxy filler and apply with a plastic squeegee or body spreader. Crown slightly and cover an area larger than the V-groove to allow the filler to be feathered out to a smooth contour.

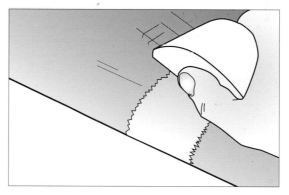

4. Allow the filler to cure as per manufacturers instructions, then sand to a smooth contour with 80- and 180-grit paper. Finish sand with 220-grit. Re-texture the area with a texture spray. Do not attempt to spot texture. Retexture and blend the leading edge or most visible area of the pad all the way across. If there is a noticeable difference in texture, then re-texture the entire dash pad.

Why Flex Concentrations in Urethane Hot-Melt Repairs Cause Problems

Urethane hot-melt adhesive is an excellent way to repair flexible and rigid thermoset urethane substrates because the bond is very strong and the urethane filler rod is very tough and flexible. Often, repairs done with urethane hot-melts are stronger than the original material.

Unfortunately, the flexibility of the urethane rod may cause problems for overlying refinish coatings and fillers. The figure here shows this effect. If the substrate is more rigid than the urethane filler rod (as it usually is), then any bending stress that is applied to the part will be concentrated in the area of the weld, rather than evenly distributed along the entire length of the part.

As a result of this flex concentration, the radius of curvature in the immediate vicinity of the repair can be quite small. This causes the outer surface of the part to stretch significantly, most often causing any overlying filler or paint layers, even flexible ones, to crack. Flexible paints and fillers are designed to bend over, say, a two-inch radius. However, if a flex concentration occurs over a urethane weld, the radius of curvature could be on the order of 1/2 inch or less.

In order to mitigate this effect, the backside of the weld repair should be reinforced with a layer

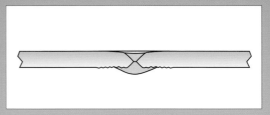

An unreinforced, unstressed urethane weld with overlying filler coat.

of two-part adhesive. This will increase the section modulus, or stiffness, of the part in the area of the repair, preventing it from concentrating so much flex along the weld line.

Flex concentration may or may not be a problem depending on part geometry. If the part is not likely to flex along the weld line due to some feature of the part that naturally supports the area, then reinforcement won't be necessary. Conversely, if the part is likely to flex along the weld line, it will be best to reinforce the backside. If this is the case, since a two-part must be used to reinforce the backside of the repair anyway, it might be preferable to use a urethane two-part repair material to do the entire repair instead of combining it with a hot-melt urethane repair. ■

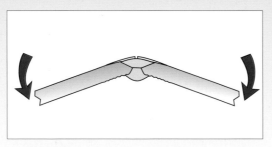

An unreinforced urethane weld subjected to bending load will concentrate all deflection along the weld line. Although the structure of the weld is not compromised, any overlying filler or paint coating will most likely crack.

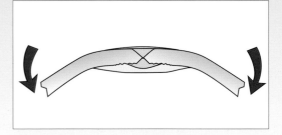

A backside reinforcement helps support the weld (via increased section modulus and a greater ability to withstand compressive forces), reducing the likelihood that the overlying coatings will crack.

onto the surface of the substrate without the risk of overheating the substrate itself.

Let's say you have a crack in a thermoset urethane panel that you want to repair. After you clean the plastic, you'll want to realign it and hold it in place while you do the hot-melt or weld repair. If the plastic panel is distorted, you can take advantage of urethane's "memory" by heating the part with a heat gun or some other source of heat as described earlier in this chapter.

Grind a V-groove halfway through the backside of the plastic using either a Dremel tool or a coarse sandpaper disc. Once again, because thermoset urethane is not meltable, you cannot melt the V-groove in with a hot tool; the V-groove must be machined in with a grinder or with sandpaper. V-grooves in urethane do not need to be very wide; 1/4 to 3/8 inch (5mm to 10mm) is sufficient.

After removing the plastic with the grinder, sand inside the V-groove and round off the sharp edges with 80-grit sandpaper. It's a good idea to sandscratch an area at least 1/4 inch on either side of the V-groove to allow for better adhesion at the edges of the hot-melt adhesive. If there is any paint in the area, remove it with sandpaper also. Once you've finished sanding the area, remove the sanding dust with clean, dry compressed air or with a clean cloth.

Now that you've finished preparing the V-groove on the backside, apply aluminum tape or use clamps to line up the damage on the frontside. Cyanoacrylate adhesive can also be useful for tacking parts together for welding if the crack fits tightly together. Once the damage is aligned and the backside is V-grooved and sanded, you're ready to begin the welding process.

Preheat the airless plastic welder to the proper temperature for the urethane welding rod as indicated on the temperature control dial. The temperature of the welder can vary during the welding process. Run a few inches of welding rod through the welder tip before applying the filler rod to the repair area. This will help stabilize the welder's temperature as it is usually slightly too hot to start with. If the welder's temperature is too hot, the urethane rod will bubble and smoke. Ideally, the rod should come out of the bottom of the welder tip melted, but clear and smooth with no bubbling. If the rod doesn't cool down slightly after running a couple inches of rod through it, reduce the temperature slightly, let the welder cool for a few minutes, then try again.

You will notice that, if the urethane rod sits in the melt tube of the welder tip for any amount of time, the urethane will start to burn and turn brown inside the hole in the tip. If you have stopped welding for any time during the welding process, it's a good idea to run an inch or so of new welding rod though the tip to clean out this dark, burned urethane.

Once you've got the temperature adjusted properly and some clean, melted urethane rod coming out from the bottom of the welding tip, it's time to apply the melted rod to the part. Holding the welder's tip slightly off the surface of the part, feed urethane rod into the welder tip with one hand while slowly moving the tip of the welder along the V-groove. Deposit enough molten welding rod into the V-groove to fill it completely and crown slightly over onto the flat area on either side of the V-groove.

Do not attempt to fill the entire length of the V-groove in one pass. It's easier to apply the urethane hot-melt in short segments, each about one to 1-1/2 inches long. The reason for this is that it's easier to smooth out the rod while it's still hot and somewhat liquid. If you do an entire six-inch crack in one pass and go back to the beginning to smooth it out, it will already be cool and hardened.

After doing a one- to 1-1/2-inch segment, remove the welding rod from the welder tip and go back over the welding rod you just deposited and smooth it out with the flat part of the welding tip. You can touch the base material with the hot welding tip briefly, but don't let the heat linger. If you overheat the thermoset urethane base material, it will break the plastic down chemically, resulting in a slippery plasticizer coming to the surface. If this happens, the only way to recover is to grind the urethane down past the heat-damaged layer into some virgin material and reapply the hot-melt.

After smoothing out the first segment of rod, run a little urethane rod through the tip onto a piece of scrap to clean out the burned material (if necessary), then repeat the process for another segment. Continue this process until you have the entire length of the V-groove on the backside filled and smoothed out.

TPO Hot Melt Cross-Sectional Repair Sequence

1.
Frontside

Backside

2.
Aluminum tape

Rough grind backside, melt in reinforcing mesh, remove gloss from melted plastic

3.
Apply universal hot melt repair rod

4.
Create v-groove with die grinder

5.
Round edges and remove paint with DA sander

6.
Fill v-groove with hot melt

7.
Sand smooth with block sander

Allow the welding rod to cool completely before working on the frontside. This usually takes about 10 minutes, but the process can be accelerated by *force cooling* the weld with water. By spraying cool water directly onto the weld or applying it with a wet sponge, you can begin working on the frontside immediately. This is one of the advantages that hot-melt adhesives have over two-parts. By force-cooling the hot-melt, you can reduce the total cycle time required to perform the repair, which is an important consideration in for-profit commercial operations.

Remove the tape on the frontside that you used to align the damage. Using a die grinder or a coarse sandpaper disc, grind a V-groove halfway through the plastic on the frontside, identical to the one you did on the back. Since you've already welded the backside, it will be hard to tell exactly when your V-groove is halfway through the plastic, so keep digging the groove in until you start getting into some of the hot-melt adhesive you applied from the other side. Again, V-grooves in urethane do not need to be very wide; 1/4 to 3/8 inch (5mm to 10mm) will be plenty.

After removing the plastic in the V-groove with the die grinder, sand inside the V-groove and round off the sharp edges with 80-grit sandpaper. With the 80-grit sandpaper, feather back the paint around the V-groove for at least 1/2 inch all around. A DA sander is good for feathering back the paint. Once you've finished sanding the area, remove the sanding dust with clean, dry compressed air or with a clean cloth.

Apply the urethane hot-melt welding rod into the V-groove using the same process that you used on the backside: weld in short segments and smooth out the rod onto the surface while the welding rod is still hot and liquid. On the frontside, it is not necessary to crown the welding rod excessively, as you will need to grind any excess material off anyway. It is better to smooth the molten rod out as flush as possible.

Force cool the hot-melt adhesive on the frontside with water or allow 10 to 15 minutes for it to cool down naturally. Because thermoplastic urethane welding rod does not feather out smoothly on the surface when sanded, you will need to cover the repaired area with a two-part filler. To do this, you'll need to grind the ure-

Repairing a Tear in TPO with Hot-Melt Repair Material

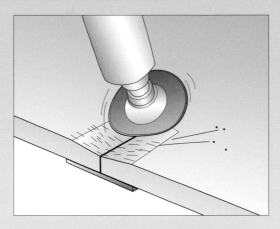

1. Grind the backside of the plastic with coarse sandpaper (50- to 80-grit) at low speed. Avoid grinding too fast as this will likely melt the plastic. Grind in a broad V-groove about halfway through the plastic if you need to finish the backside cosmetically. If not, simply grind the plastic flat. Blow dust-free.

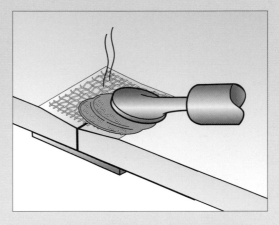

2. If desired, melt stainless steel reinforcing mesh directly into the plastic across the crack. This is usually only necessary if the plastic is torn to the edge and additional strength is necessary. After melting the mesh in, allow the plastic to cool and resolidify.

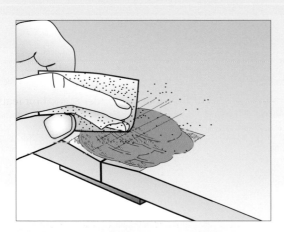

3. Remove the gloss from the melted plastic using 50-grit sandpaper by hand. The hot-melt repair material will not stick to a glossy surface, so put some sandscratches into the plastic first. It's better not to use a power tool here as it will likely be too aggressive and may actually start to rip the reinforcement out of the plastic.

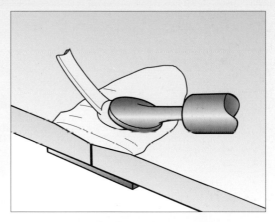

4. Using an airless plastic welder at the highest temperature setting, melt the hot-melt repair material onto the surface and spread it smoothly over the prepared area using the hot welder tip. Do not attempt to melt the rod with the base material. Simply melt the rod and spread it over the base material. Feather the hot-melt together with the base only around the edges. Allow the repair material on the backside to cool completely.

(cont. on next page)

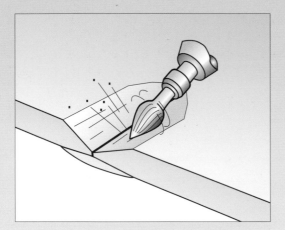

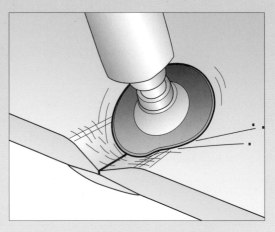

5. On the frontside, create a wide V-groove with a die grinder. The V-groove should go all the way through the plastic, or should meet the V-groove ground in other side. If you were to look at a cross section of the area, the base material should taper down to a point at the crack. The V-groove should have a total width of one to two inches.

6. Grind the V-groove with coarse sandpaper (50- to 80-grit). Sandscratch completely leaving no glossy surface visible. Round off the edges of the V-groove with 80-grit sandpaper in a DA sander and remove paint for about 1/2 inch all around the V-groove. Use 180-grit paper for this if the plastic is unpainted, textured TPO. Blow dust-free.

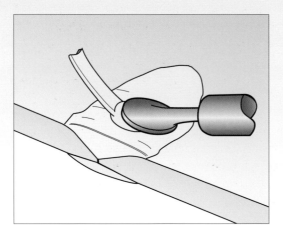

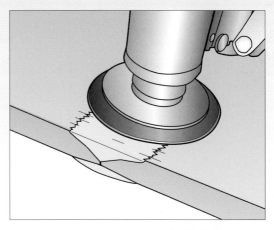

7. Melt the hot-melt repair material into the V-groove and spread it smoothly over the prepared area using the hot welder tip. Slightly overfill the V-groove to allow for finish sanding. Do not attempt to melt the rod with the base material. Simply melt the rod and spread it over the base material. Feather the hot-melt together with the base only around the edges.

8. After allowing the repair material to cool completely, rough sand the cosmetic side with 80-grit in a DA sander at low speed. Avoid sanding at high speed as the friction heat generated will likely soften the repair material. Fill any low spots with more hot-melt repair material or with a skim coat of two-part filler. Finish sand with 180- and 220-grit prior to refinishing.

thane welding rod slightly flush with a coarse sandpaper, then skim coat with the two-part filler of your choice. Epoxy two-parts are easier to sand than urethane two-parts, so they are the product of choice for this type of application. The procedure for applying cosmetic fillers is described in detail earlier in this chapter.

There is one area of caution that must be observed when doing urethane hot-melt repairs on thermoset urethane substrates. Because the thermoplastic urethane welding rod is usually more flexible than the substrate to which it is applied, if the part is flexed, the deformation of the part may be concentrated in the repair area. The more rigid the substrate, the more this effect is magnified. If the deformation is concentrated in the repair area, the radius of curvature will be smaller than any overlying paint or filler material layer can withstand, causing the paint or filler material to crack. Structurally, the repair will be sound, but cosmetically, the repair will be considered a failure.

To address this problem, you will need to apply a patch of two-part adhesive on the backside of the part to support the welded area. By increasing the cross-sectional thickness of the part in the repair area, the tendency to concentrate the deformation at the weld line will be reduced. A urethane two-part material is the best choice for creating a backing patch as its flexibility will most closely match that of the base material.

This is not necessarily going to be a problem, as it depends not only on the flexibility of the substrate but on the part's geometry as well. If other features in the part's geometry support the welded area, then reinforcement will not be necessary. For example, if the tear is a vertical gash in the middle of a car's bumper, it would be impossible for the part to bend such that the deformation would be along the weld line.

If you determine that the weld will probably need a backing reinforcement anyway, it will probably save you time to do the entire repair with a two-part urethane adhesive. If, however, you determine that the weld will probably not need a backing reinforcement, welding the repair with a hot-melt urethane will probably be faster and less expensive than a two-part urethane repair.

Repairing Polyolefin Thermoplastics with Hot-Melt Repair Materials

Most thermoplastics are easy to repair because you have a variety of repair options, including fusion welding, to choose from. Rigid plastics like PC and ABS are the easiest to repair because any adhesive—two-part, CA, or methacrylate—can repair them. The most troublesome thermoplastics to repair, however, are the polyolefins.

Polyolefins are a class of plastics that feature long chains of carbon and hydrogen atoms (i.e., hydrocarbons) with no ring structures. The mono-olefins—ethylene and propylene—are derived directly from petroleum distillation, which gives the resulting polyolefins—polyethylene and polypropylene—their characteristic oily feel and appearance.

This inherent oiliness makes it very difficult for adhesives to stick to their surfaces. As a result, fusion welding is often the only way to repair straight polyethylene or polypropylene. Fortunately, both of these plastics weld very easily. Unfortunately, most polyolefins used on cars and motorcycles are not straight, but rather alloys of polypropylene, synthetic rubber, and other plastics.

These alloys, commonly known as TPO (thermoplastic olefin) or TEO (thermoplastic elastomer olefinic), are easy to fusion weld if a compatible filler rod is available. The problem is that there are hundreds, if not thousands, of different alloys of TPO made by dozens of different manufacturers, and no two are exactly the same. It is most likely that a straight PP welding rod would not work well for fusion welding a given TPO. Likewise, it is very unlikely that a matching welding rod would be commercially available.

Fortunately, there are thermoplastic hot-melt repair materials on the market that provide good adhesion to polyolefins, so even if a matching fusion welding rod cannot be found, an adequate, and often superior, repair can be performed with the hot-melt adhesive.

Thermoplastic hot-melt repair materials are designed to work best on TPO plastics since they are the most challenging type of plastic to repair in the automotive field. Because of their low surface energy, however, they will wet out and stick to a wide variety of substrates. Therefore, hot-melts can be used to repair plastics such as rigid thermoplastics and flexible thermoset urethanes. There are often other easier and faster ways to repair these plastics, however.

To perform a hot-melt adhesive repair on a crack in a TPO part, first clean the plastic. Align the torn edges together using an aluminum-backed body tape, clamps, or some other means. You may also remove or minimize any distortions in the plastic using a heat gun.

Like any adhesive, a thermoplastic hot-melt adhesive will stick better to a surface that is roughed up, so grind the backside of the plastic for at least one inch all around the crack with a coarse sandpaper (50- to 80-grit). On a microscopic scale, sandscratching the plastic will vastly increase the total surface area for the hot-melt to stick to.

On TPOs, and polyolefins in general, do not sand or grind the plastic with high-speed, air-powered tools. These tools are very common in body shops and are great time savers when working on metals and thermoset plastics. However, they usually spin so fast that the friction heat created by the sandpaper on the surface is enough to melt and smear a thermoplastic substrate. Polyolefins are particularly susceptible to this since they have low melting points.

I strongly recommend the use of a low-speed electric grinder, like an angle drill, when working on TPO. Electric tools have high torque at low speed and can thus put a nice sandscratch into the surface with no risk of melting the plastic. By contrast, air-powered tools have almost no torque at low speed and are almost impossible to throttle down slow enough to grind in a proper V-groove.

This results in one of the most common errors made by technicians during the preparation of a TPO substrate for repair. The technician will whip out his trusty old air grinder, put a 50-grit sandpaper disc on it, spin it up to 20,000 rpm, and lay it down on the plastic. The friction heat generated simply melts the plastic and smears it away. The technician will then presume that he has completed the preparation step properly because he *sanded* the plastic. What he has actually done is *melt* the plastic. If you looked at the surface through a microscope, it would be smooth. Even without a microscope, the surface will look shinier than a surface that has been properly sanded at low speed. Obviously, the problem is that if the plastic is shiny and smooth, the subsequent repair material used will not stick well to the surface. In such a case, the technician will usually blame the adhesive because he "sanded the plastic" just like the instructions told him to. The importance of proper surface preparation when repairing plastics, especially polyolefins, cannot be overemphasized.

If you can build up a thickness or patch on the backside of the plastic without a problem, simply grind the backside of the plastic flat with no V-groove. If, for cosmetic reasons, you need to sand or finish the backside of the part, grind a V-groove halfway through the part with a die grinder first, then grind inside the V-groove with the coarse sandpaper. When using a hot-melt repair material, the V-groove should be broad, say 1-1/2 to 2 inches wide total (3/4 to 1 inch on each side of the crack). Scratch up the plastic surrounding the V-groove as well. A simple rule is to sandscratch any place where you plan to apply the adhesive. Once you've finished sanding, remove the sanding dust and chips with clean, dry compressed air or a clean cloth.

Before applying the hot-melt adhesive, you have an opportunity to reinforce the crack with stainless steel wire mesh if necessary. This is an especially effective way to increase the strength of the repair beyond that even of a fusion weld repair. By melting stainless-steel wire mesh into the TPO substrate across the crack, you allow any stresses in the part to be transferred across the crack directly into the substrate. You are in essence creating a composite structure similar to that of concrete; steel rebar takes the tensile loads while the concrete substrate takes the compressive loads.

Reinforcing mesh is not always necessary, however. If the tear is in the middle of the part where it will not likely be distorted or bent, using the mesh would be superfluous. But if the tear extends to the edge of the part, the mesh can make a great contribution to the strength of the finished repair. The mesh is also very useful for fabricating missing tabs and filling holes. By

Repairing a Torn Mounting Hole in TPO with Hot-Melt Repair Material

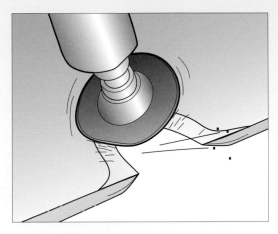

1. Grind the plastic in a generous area around the torn mounting hole on both sides with coarse sandpaper (50- to 80-grit) in a rotary grinder at low speed. Taper the plastic to a point at the edges. This will maximize the area over which the hot-melt repair material can adhere, creating a stronger repair.

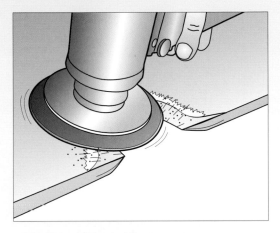

2. Remove any paint in an area about 1/2 inch outside of the taper with 80-grit sandpaper in a DA sander. Use the 80-grit to rough up the repair taper created in the first step to further increase the surface area available for adhesion. Blow dust-free with clean, dry, compressed air.

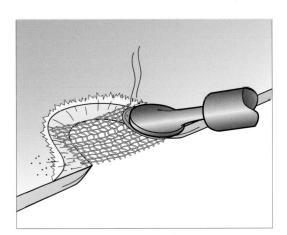

3. If desired, melt stainless steel reinforcing mesh into the plastic across the gap. Make sure mesh is buried into taper so it is not exposed later during finish sanding. The mesh may cover the bolt hole since the hole will need to be drilled out later anyway.

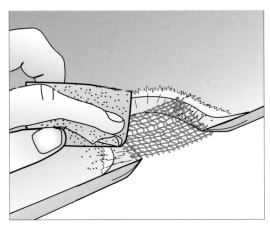

4. After the melted plastic cools, remove the shine from the surface by sanding by hand with coarse sandpaper. Blow dust-free. If mesh is not used, apply aluminum-backed tape across the gap on the backside to support the welding rod while it is molten.

(cont. on next page)

Repairing a Torn Mounting Hole in TPO
with Hot-Melt Repair Material (Cont.)

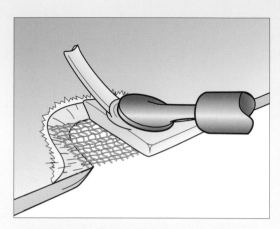

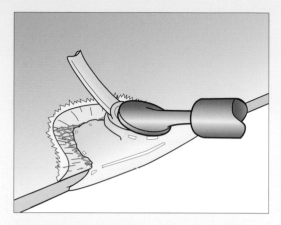

5. Using the hot-airless welder tip, melt the repair material onto the surface and spread it across the repair taper. Hot-melt repair material should not be melted with the base material; rather, it should be spread onto the surface. Slight melting of the base material is acceptable at the outside edge where the repair material is smoothed out and feathered with the base. For maximum strength, completely fill the original bolt hole.

6. After the repair material cools on one side, repeat the application process on the other side. Avoid building up too much material as most bolt flanges can't be built up on the backside for extra strength as can most other repairs. Allow repair material to cool completely.

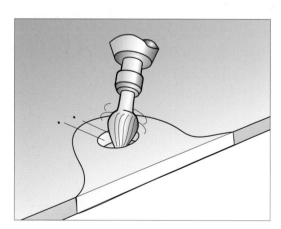

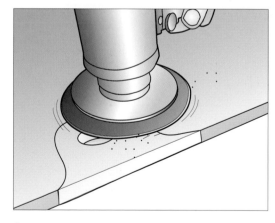

7. Drill out the bolt hole. After opening up the hole with a twist drill bit, use a die grinder to achieve the hole's final dimensions or to create an oval shape, as necessary.

8. Sand both sides with 80-grit paper in a DA sander at low speed. Feather the repair material out with the base material at the edges. Fill any low spots in with more hot-melt repair material as desired. Finish sand the cosmetic side with 180-, 220-, and 320-grit sandpaper before refinishing.

melting a patch of the mesh across the hole on the backside, the mesh creates a structure to which the hot-melt repair material can stick.

To reinforce the repair with wire mesh, use scissors to trim the mesh to the proper size. For cracks, a width of about 3/4 inch is good. The mesh does not have to cover the entire length of the crack. If you are mainly concerned about reinforcing the area near the edge, then implanting the mesh near the edge should be sufficient. If you are really concerned about the strength, you may also leave a portion of the mesh hanging off the edge, which will allow you to wrap the mesh around and melt it into the V-groove on the frontside as well. This will provide maximum reinforcement to the stress point at the edge of the plastic where cracking is most likely to begin.

Position the mesh where you want it and, with the welder set on the highest heat setting, press it down into the plastic with the hot welder tip. Press it just under the surface, not more than a quarter of the way through the plastic. After you lift the welder tip up, you'll notice that the melted plastic has been displaced around the outside edge of the welder tip. Use the welder tip to move this melted plastic back over the mesh.

Before moving the welding tip to another spot on the mesh, allow the first spot to cool enough for the plastic to solidify. If you are in a hurry, use a screwdriver or some other tool to press the mesh down into the first spot while you press another spot with the welder tip. If you press on another spot of the mesh without holding the first spot down with a tool, the mesh is likely to pop up out of the melted plastic in the first spot. The end result you want to achieve is to have the mesh evenly buried into the plastic on the backside.

After melting the mesh in, allow the plastic to solidify. It doesn't have to be completely cool, just solid. Then scratch the newly melted plastic by hand with a coarse (50-grit) sandpaper. After melting the plastic, it will have a smooth and shiny surface. Just as before, you need to remove the shine and put some sandscratches into the plastic to give the hot-melt repair material something to stick to. It is best to sand by hand to minimize damage to the mesh by the sandpaper. If an electric or air grinder is used to scratch the plas-

tic, you're likely to start ripping up the wires in the mesh that you just implanted.

The next step is to apply the hot-melt repair material to the backside. First of all, hot-melts are always applied with an airless plastic welder, not a hot-air welder. Because hot-melts have an extremely short *open,* or working time, they need to be melted and spread onto the surface at the same

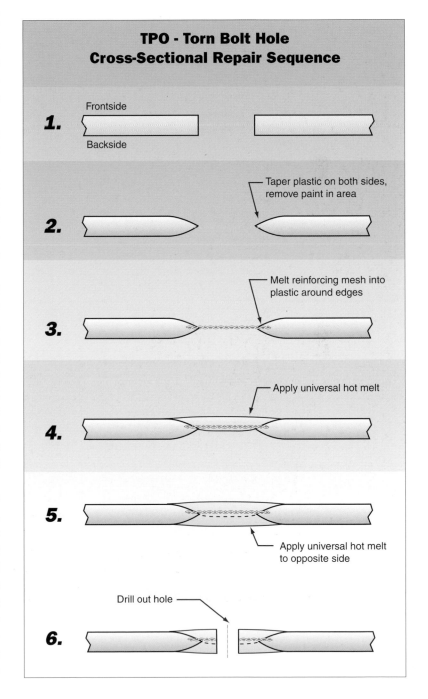

TPO - Torn Bolt Hole Cross-Sectional Repair Sequence

1. Frontside / Backside

2. Taper plastic on both sides, remove paint in area

3. Melt reinforcing mesh into plastic around edges

4. Apply universal hot melt

5. Apply universal hot melt to opposite side

6. Drill out hole

time. Most hot-air welders have a jet of hot air, which will melt the hot-melt but not spread it.

The application process will differ depending on the type of rod you are using. There are two types of hot-melt rods: round and flat. The round rod is used with a welding tip with a hole in it, which the rod is fed through. The application process using a round hot-melt adhesive will be identical to that used for a urethane hot-melt repair as described in this chapter. You simply feed the rod slowly through the hot welder tip, allowing it to melt as it goes through. The melted rod is dispensed or extruded onto the surface and, while it is still molten, spread over the surface.

The flat welding rod is used with a flat, round welding tip, approximately 3/4-inch diameter. The application process is a little slower and more complicated than the process with the round rod. Holding the rod in one hand and the welder in the other, melt one side of a small section (about one to 1-1/2 inches long) at the tip of the rod. Before the rod has a chance to cool, immediately put the melted side down onto the prepared substrate. Cut off the section of rod that is stuck to the plastic with the edge of your welder tip, then immediately melt this section completely and spread it onto the surface. For proper adhesion, it is very important to make sure the part of the rod that is put down onto the plastic is melted.

Using either method, melt and spread the hot-melt repair material on the backside of the plastic over the prepared area. Just as with the urethane hot-melt repair method, it is best to immediately smooth out each small section of weld rod you deposit while the rod is still melted. If you go back and try to smooth the repair material out after it cools off, it will take longer and the results won't be as attractive. At the edges of the repair material, use the welder's tip to feather the rod smoothly with the base material. It's okay if the heat of the welder melts the base material slightly, especially if the substrate is a TPO. Thermoplastic hot-melts are usually polyolefin-based and, thus, very compatible with the substrate, so a slight amount of fusion with the base material is acceptable.

Before continuing the repair process on the frontside, the repair material on the backside

needs to cool sufficiently. You may allow it to cool naturally for five to ten minutes or quick cool it with water. Because the repair material is thermoplastic, there is no need to allow time for a chemical reaction to take place like thermoset two-parts require. As soon as the thermoplastic repair material is cool, it will have attained its final strength. This ability to quick cool a hot-melt repair can significantly reduce the cycle time required to complete the repair.

Once the repair on the backside has attained handling strength, you can peel the tape off the front or remove the clamps you used to fixture the part together during the backside repair. If you ground the backside of the plastic flat, then you'll want to grind a broad V-groove on the front that extends all the way through the plastic. If you V-grooved the plastic on the backside, then you'll want your frontside V-groove to extend through until it touches the backside V-groove.

Remember, when preparing a V-groove for a hot-melt repair material, the width should be generous, say one to two inches wide total (1/2 to one inch on each side of the crack). Because you'll have to remove a fair amount of plastic to create the V-groove, it is easier to shape the channel with a carbide-tipped burr in a high-speed air die grinder. Grinding the whole V-groove in with coarse sandpaper is more time consuming, leading to the risk that you'll lose patience with the process before it is done properly.

If you use a die grinder to create the V-groove, the preparation will not be complete until you put some sandscratches inside the plastic with some coarse sandpaper. This is another mistake technicians often make. They assume that since they just hogged out a big channel in the plastic with an air die grinder, they roughed it up. However, if you look closely at the surface created by a carbide burr, it's actually very smooth. If it's sharp, the burr has likely removed the plastic in big chips and if it's dull, the burr has probably melted the plastic. Either way, neither surface is adequate to provide adhesion for the repair material. If the technician attempts to apply the hot-melt repair material to this surface, it will likely not stick when sanded and especially

Applying Flat-Stick Hot-Melt Repair Material

Hot-melt repair materials come in two formats: flat sticks and continuous round rods. The round rod is melted using a special welding tip that allows the rod to be fed through and melted in a continuous process. The melting process for round hot-melt rod would be identical to that used for urethane hot-melt repair material.

Flat-stick hot-melts are a bit more complicated. In order to get proper adhesion to the base material, the surface of the hot-melt rod that first touches the substrate should already be melted. If the flat stick is simply laid onto the surface and melted from the top, the bottom side of the rod may not melt completely, thus causing adhesion problems. In order to get proper adhesion of a flat-stick hot-melt rod, use the following procedure. ■

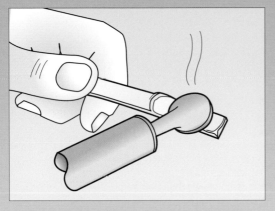

1. Hold the flat welding rod close to the end above the repair area. Use the hot welding tip to pre-melt one side of the welding rod for a length of about 1/2 to 3/4 inch. The rod should be thoroughly melted about halfway through its thickness.

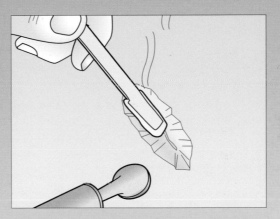

2. Immediately stick the melted side of the rod onto the prepared repair area.

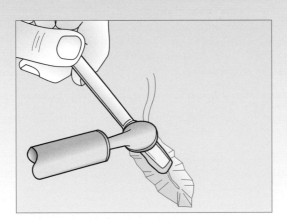

3. Nip off the short segment of rod that is sticking to the plastic with the edge of the welder tip.

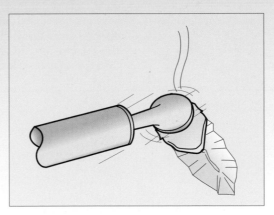

4. Use the hot welder tip to melt the top side of the rod segment and spread it over the repair area as desired. Repeat this process to continue filling the repair taper.

Applying Methacrylate Adhesive with Mix Method

Methacrylate Adhesive Mix Ratio vs. Working Time				
Mix Ratio	Liquid	1 part	2 parts	3 parts
	Powder	1 part	1 part	1 part
Working Time		30 sec to 1 min	1 min to 3 min	2 min to 7 min

Mixing the methacrylate monomer and polymer prior to application is the easiest and fastest way to apply the adhesive. The powder may be blended with one to three parts liquid in a small cup; the more liquid used, the longer it takes for the material to gel, thus increasing the working time. The material will get more and more viscous as time goes on, so you can wait to apply the material until the viscosity is just right for the application in question. A thinner adhesive is more suited to pouring and casting, while a thicker adhesive is better for spreading onto vertical surfaces. The only disadvantage to this application method is the porosity that occurs within the material as the bulk quantity polymerizes. If appearance is of primary importance, the needle dropper method is preferred. ■

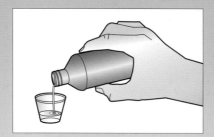

1. Pour liquid monomer into polypropylene or polyethylene plastic cup (styrene-based cups will dissolve very quickly). The volume of liquid used can be adjusted to suit the total amount of adhesive needed and the working time required. To a certain point, the more liquid used, the longer the working time (see table). Try using a 2:1 liquid-to-powder ratio at first.

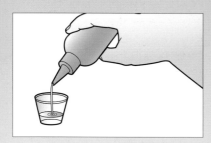

2. Pour methacrylate polymer powder into liquid in the proper proportion. Exact measurements are not required.

3. Mix the powder and liquid together until uniform. More powder may be added to thicken the liquid, but be cautioned that this may thicken the adhesive more quickly than you can react to it. Adding more liquid will not thin the adhesive out again. It is better to simply wait until the material thickens naturally than to add more powder.

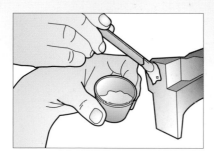

4. When the adhesive reaches the consistency desired, apply to the prepared area. If working on a vertical area, you can cover the material with a polyethylene film (for example, a sheet cut from a Ziploc bag) to keep it from sagging before it sets up. The material will be hard enough to sand or drill in about an hour.

if it is picked at. This leads the technician to assume that the product is no good because he did everything the directions said and it still didn't stick. I cannot overemphasize how important a properly prepared surface is to a good plastic repair, especially when working with TPOs. With slippery plastics like TPO, there is very little margin for error in the surface preparation stage.

To obtain good adhesion, use a coarse sandpaper disc (50- to 80-grit) in a slow speed electric grinder or angle drill to completely roughen the plastic inside the V-groove. Before you start using the coarse sandpaper to grind the area around the V-groove as well, take caution. More care must be taken in sanding on the frontside than on the back since you're likely going to be refinishing or painting the outer surface. For example, if you're repairing an unpainted, textured TPO (a popular finish for many car bumper covers), don't scratch the area surrounding the V-groove with anything coarser than 180-grit paper. Deep scratches in the area surrounding the V-groove are nearly impossible to hide with the refinishing techniques used for these types of bumpers.

Even on painted TPO surfaces, it is a good idea to not use anything coarser than 80-grit to scratch the paint off in the area surrounding the V-groove. TPO is a soft plastic that will scratch deeply, and deep scratches are more difficult to hide later on. Remove the paint in an area about 1/2 inch surrounding the V-groove and round off the sharp edge leading into the V-groove with 80- or 120-grit paper in a DA sander. For the best featheredge of the repair material in the end, you want to create a smooth, evenly radiused transition from the V-groove onto the flat outer surface.

After you've obtained a good, even sandscratch over the entire area, remove the sanding dust with clean, dry compressed air or a clean cloth. If you decide to clean the plastic at this stage with a plastic cleaning solvent, make sure you allow plenty of time for the solvents to evaporate from all the tiny scratches you've created, or, preferably, heat the area lightly with a heat gun to accelerate the evaporation process. Again, if you did the cleaning properly in the first place, there is no reason to clean again at this stage and, if you don't evaporate all the solvents, you may cause yourself even greater problems by cleaning.

Using the same process you used on the backside, apply the hot-melt repair material inside the V-groove on the frontside. Crown the adhesive slightly and smooth it out around the edges onto the flat area surrounding the V-groove. Melt a small amount of the repair material onto the surface at a time and smooth it out while it is still molten and hot. Use the hot welder tip to feather the edge of the repair material out even with the base material surrounding the V-groove.

Once the V-groove is filled with repair material and smoothed out to your satisfaction, allow it to cool completely. Again, you can accelerate this process with water or a wet sponge. Don't begin sanding the hot-melt repair material until it is completely cool.

Begin sanding with 80- or 120-grit paper, or 180-grit if you are working on an unpainted, textured TPO part. Once you get close to the final profile, switch to 180- or 220-grit and feather the repair material out onto the flat area around the V-groove. As long as the preparation steps and the welding process were done properly, the repair material should feather out onto the plastic very well. If you see that the featheredge is lifting or breaking off in small chunks around the outside edge, you have a problem. If it's just in a small area, you might be able to dig it out with coarse sandpaper and reapply the hot-melt in that area. If the featheredge is lifting all over, you'll have to grind it all out and start over, taking even more care during the preparation steps and perhaps cleaning after grinding.

Once in a while, despite doing everything properly, the repair material may still lift. This is most likely due to the formulation of the base material itself and no fault of yours. As you recall, there are hundreds of different formulations of TPO on the market, and some are slipperier than others. Some TPOs are also blended with mold release agents (i.e., oils) throughout the material, making adhesion to the plastic that much tougher. In the very rare case that you can't get an adhesive to feather on a TPO part despite your best efforts, it would be best to abandon the attempt and buy a replacement part.

Assuming that the repair material feathers out nicely, you may be left with some low spots that were not filled in the original application of the repair material. There are two ways to fill these spots. You can dab on small amounts of hot-melt repair material into the low spots, or give the entire area a skim coat with a two-part epoxy. If you have other imperfections on the part that you were planning to fill with two-part anyway, it would be faster to skim over your repair area at the same time. If you have only a small, isolated area to repair and the rest of the part looks good, it would probably be faster to dab on some more hot-melt.

If you fill the low spots with more hot-melt, you don't need to sand the shiny spots out of the existing hot-melt as they will melt together when you apply the new filler material. If you fill the low spots with a two-part, you'll need to sandscratch any shiny spots by hand to allow the two-part to get adhesion to the hot-melt. Also, depending on the two-part repair material you use, you may also need to apply an adhesion promoter to the surface first. Check the application instructions for your two-part and follow the instructions for cosmetic two-part repairs.

Repairing Rigid Plastics with Methacrylate Adhesives

There is a relatively new plastic repair technology that uses methylmethacrylate monomer to create a strong repair on many rigid plastics. Going by trade names such as PlastiFix, Plastex, and Plast-Aid, this repair system is used by mixing a liquid methylmethacrylate monomer with a powdered catalyst. The catalyst causes the monomer to polymerize, creating a solid material.

Unlike all other two-part adhesives used for plastic repair, the methacrylate adhesive does not form a crosslinked thermoset material. Instead, the polymerization reaction forms a thermo*plastic* polymethylmethacrylate, or PMMA, a.k.a. acrylic, the same stuff that is used to make taillight lenses and the like. In other words, the resultant "adhesive" is actually a thermoplastic acrylic.

The adhesion of methacrylate adhesives varies depending on the substrate. They stick very well to acrylics, styrenes (ABS), polycarbonates, SMC, and fiberglass substrates. They stick less well to polyester and nylon, but can still be used for non-stressed applications. They do not stick at all to polyolefin substrates (PE, PP, and TPO).

Methacrylate adhesives have some capabilities that are unique among all available adhesive technologies. First, because they are acrylic, they can offer very good visual clarity, allowing repairs to be done on headlight and taillight lenses. Second, some of the methacrylate adhesive kits available come with flexible molding bars that allow you to duplicate details and replace tabs and other features that may be missing from the part. This is an especially useful aspect for the repair of street bike fairings as they often have easily breakable tabs and flanges.

Methacrylate adhesives consist of a water-thin liquid monomer and a powdered catalyst. If the catalyst is saturated with the liquid, the polymerization reaction will start. There are three ways of combining the powder and liquid depending on the geometry and orientation of the part you want to repair. Because the water-thin monomer will run downhill before it gels with the powder, it is very helpful if the part can be removed so that the damaged area may be oriented horizontally.

First, the liquid and powder may be mixed in a cup and applied to the surface with a trowel or poured into a cast once it reaches the proper viscosity. The mixing ratio may vary from 1:1 to 3:1 liquid-to-powder on a volume basis. The more liquid is used, the longer it will take for the mixture to gel, allowing more working time. This application method works well for both horizontally and vertically oriented damage. If horizontal, the mixture may be poured in place, and if vertical the mixture may be allowed to gel sufficiently to hang onto the vertical surface.

A second way of applying the material is to sprinkle thin layers of the powder directly onto the surface then saturating with the monomer; obviously, the damaged area must be oriented horizontally. This method works well when reinforcing the backside of a damaged area with fiberglass cloth.

The third and final way of applying a methacrylate adhesive is with a needle dropper.

Applying Methacrylate Adhesive and Reinforcing by Direct Application Method

When covering a broad area with a methacrylate adhesive, it is often desirable to use the direct application method. In this case, the polymer powder is sprinkled directly onto the surface and then saturated with the liquid monomer. This process is repeated in thin layers to achieve the final desired thickness. This method avoids the bulk curing reaction which causes porosity in the mix method of application. It can only be used on horizontal surfaces, however.

This sequence shows how a crack may be reinforced by creating a composite structure with fiberglass cloth encased in the methacrylate polymer as applied by the direct application method. ■

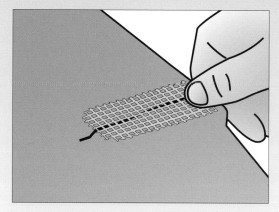

1. Sand the area over which the adhesive will be applied with coarse sandpaper and blow dust-free. Cut fiberglass cloth to cover the damaged area on the backside. The cloth should lap over the edges of the crack or hole about 1/2 inch.

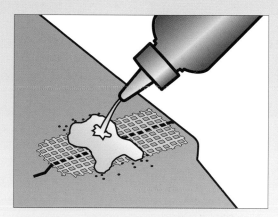

2. Sprinkle a thin layer of methacrylate powder over the area. If the powder is applied too thick, the liquid may not soak all the way through.

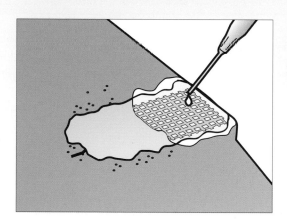

3. Saturate the powder with liquid monomer. Repeat the process of sprinkling powder and applying liquid until the desired thickness is achieved.

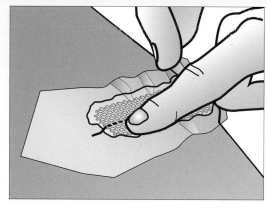

4. Cover the area with clear polyethylene film (as cut from a Ziploc bag, for example). Press the material to shape and remove any air bubbles with your fingers. Allow the adhesive to cure completely (about one hour) before peeling off the plastic film.

Applying Methacrylate Adhesive with Dropper Method

There are three basic methods for applying methacrylate adhesives, each having its advantages for a given damage geometry. The needle dropper method allows for very precise location of the adhesive, which is an advantage for filling areas that have intricate detail. The dropper method also minimizes the porosity that occurs when the exothermic polymerization reaction begins, resulting in a better finished appearance. The disadvantage of this method is that it is slower than the other methods. ■

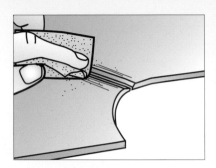

1. Prepare the surface by creating a V-groove or taper with a die grinder, then sand inside the groove and in the surrounding area with 80-grit sandpaper. Roughing up the plastic first will maximize the surface area over which the adhesive may stick.

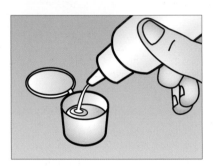

2. Fill the cup with powder and the needle applicator bottle with liquid. The drops are easier to form and control if both bottle and cup are nearly full of material.

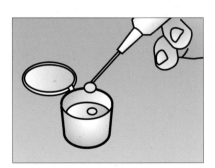

3. Hold the needle just above the surface of the powder and squeeze one or two drops of liquid into the powder. Squeezing out more than two drops of liquid will make too large of a powder/liquid ball, making it difficult to pick up.Immediately stab and pick up the drop of liquid with the tip of the needle. If the drop is not too heavy, it should cling to the end of the needle via surface tension.

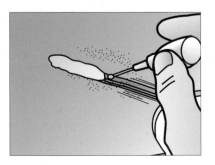

4. Move the powder/liquid ball over the area where you want to apply it. Squeezing a little more liquid out will wash the powder/liquid ball off the tip and onto the repair area. (The hole in the needle is not at the tip, but rather halfway up the shaft, allowing the liquid to easily wash the material off the tip.) Repeat this process until the repair area is filled to your satisfaction.

Using this method, a drop or two of the monomer is dropped into a cup of powder using a needle applicator. The needle is immediately used to stab and pick up the drop of liquid. The drop will hang onto the tip of the needle by surface tension. The drop is then moved over the area of application, then washed off the tip with another squirt of liquid. This method allows very precise placement of the adhesive. However, because the viscosity of the material is low when it is applied, it is better to have the damaged area oriented horizontally.

Detailed instructions regarding how to apply the methacrylate adhesive using each of these methods are shown in the accompanying sidebars. Regardless of which method of application is used, the preparation steps are the same. First, align and clean the plastic according to instructions given earlier in this chapter.

Second, like for most other adhesives, the surface should be sandscratched to maximize the surface area to which the adhesive can stick. A coarse sandpaper, like 80-grit, should be used for this step. The damaged area should also be generously tapered or V-grooved to allow space for the adhesive to stick after the surface is smoothed.

Finally, remove the sanding dust with clean, dry compressed air or a clean cloth. After sanding, don't clean the area again with a plastic cleaning solution. Adhesion is not a problem on the types of plastics that methacrylates will stick to, so the extra cleaning step is not necessary and may actually cause problems if all the solvents are not properly evaporated before applying the adhesive. All you want is a clean, dry, tapered, and sandscratched surface for the methacrylate adhesive to stick to.

Once the methacrylate adhesive is mixed and applied, the speed of its cure depends on the proportion of powder to liquid. Assuming at least that all the powder is saturated with the liquid, the more powder in the mix, the faster the monomer will polymerize (i.e., cure). However, if not enough powder is used, the monomer may never fully polymerize. Again, the mix ratio should be between 1:1 to 3:1 liquid-to-powder. If mixed within this range, the methacrylate will be hard enough to sand in 30 to 90 minutes.

One thing to be cautious of when mixing the liquid and powder together in bulk is that the polymerization reaction is exothermic; in other words, it puts off heat. If the methacrylate is poured into a thick cross section, the heat generated from the reaction will actually boil the liquid, creating air bubbles in the resultant solid material. If visual clarity is important, as it would be on a headlight lens repair, for example, use the dropper method of application as this spreads out the reaction over time, minimizing the risk of overheating.

Repairing Cracks with Methacrylate Adhesives

When repairing cracks with methacrylate adhesives, V-groove the plastic halfway through on both sides using a die grinder. Round off the edges of the V-groove with 80-grit sandpaper and sand out onto the flat area surrounding the crack. Blow the area dust-free, then tape or clamp the cracked parts together to line up the damage on the outer (cosmetic) surface.

Apply the methacrylate adhesive to the backside first using any of the three application methods described. The dropper method works well for filling the V-groove, but can be time consuming if the crack is long. If the crack is long, mix the powder and liquid in a cup and pour or spread it into the crack while it is still quite liquid.

After filling the crack itself, the area can be reinforced with fiberglass cloth. First, cut a piece of woven cloth about 3/4 inch wide for the length of the crack. Make sure the plastic is sandscratched over the entire area over which the cloth will lay, plus some. Wet the area with the monomer first, then sprinkle a thin layer of powder over the wetted area. Wet any powder that remains dry with more monomer, then lay the prepared piece of fiberglass cloth over the area.

Wet the fiberglass with more monomer, then sprinkle powder on top of that. Repeat this process until you've built up a sufficient layer of methacrylate adhesive over the fiberglass cloth. Finally, lay a piece of clear plastic film (possibly cut from a Ziploc bag) over the area and smooth out the air bubbles with your fingers. Leave the plastic film on top of the adhesive until it has polymerized. When the film is finally peeled off, you will have a strong acrylic-glass composite patch to support the repair on the backside.

Peel off the tape on the frontside and fill the frontside V-groove with methacrylate adhesive like you did on the back. The front may also be reinforced with glass as long as a channel is cut down into the plastic to provide room for the cloth. When the methacrylate adhesive has cured completely, it may be sanded to a smooth contour. There will usually be a small imperfection at the featheredge, so if you want a perfect cosmetic appearance, it is best to sand the area slightly flush and apply a skim coat of two-part epoxy filler over the area.

Repairing Broken Tabs with Methacrylate Adhesives

Some of the methacrylate adhesive kits come with a flexible plastic molding bar that can be used to create a mold, allowing you to recast or recreate plastic features that are completely missing or lost. Assuming that you have another feature on the part that is identical or similar, you can create a mold using this unbroken feature, transfer the mold to the broken area, and then fill the mold with methacrylate adhesive.

The molding bars are normally heated in hot water for a few minutes until they soften. The softened bar is pulled from the water and immediately shaped around the unbroken pattern by hand. The molding material is allowed to cool while it is wrapped around the pattern, then peeled off. The resulting mold can then be filled in place with methacrylate adhesive. Silly Putty can also be used to create a mold, although Silly Putty is deformable at room temperature and can more easily be accidentally distorted.

Before attaching the mold in the damaged area, the surface needs to be tapered with 80-grit sandpaper to maximize the total surface area over which the adhesive will be applied. Proper surface preparation is essential to getting a strong repair. Once the surface is properly prepared, the mold can be taped in location and filled with the adhesive. After the adhesive has cured, it can be drilled and sanded to final shape.

Restoring Stripped Threads with Methacrylate Adhesives

One unique thing you can do with methacrylate adhesives is repair stripped screw threads. The process is very simple. First, drill or file the stripped threads out so that the screw is quite loose in the hole. There needs to be sufficient space between the screw and the hole for the adhesive to exist.

Apply oil directly to the threads of the screw to act as a mold release agent. A light motor oil or a spray-on lubricant like WD-40 or Liquid Wrench works well for this. Make sure the bottom face of the screw or bolt head is also coated with oil.

Using the dropper or mix method, apply the methacrylate mixture directly to the screw threads, then immediately drop the screw into the hole while the adhesive is wet. Allow at least one hour for the adhesive to cure, then you'll be able to unthread the screw. This process literally casts the screw threads back in place right inside the hole. You'll notice that the screw will take more torque to turn than normal. That's because the clearance that normally exists between the male and female threads is not there, because you've cast the female threads in place directly with the male threads. This tighter fit is usually not a problem unless the screw has to be removed and replaced often.

Introduction to Plastic Welding

Most plastic repairs are done with adhesives, as opposed to welding, for good reason. Adhesives tend to be simpler to use, they are less dependent on proper identification of the plastic, and they don't require an investment in welding equipment up front. If you're interested only in doing the occasional repair, the wide variety of available adhesives will allow you to repair virtually any plastic.

However, if you are interested in doing more than the just occasional repair, or if you're faced with the repair of a polyethylene or TPO substrate, making the investment in a plastic welder will pay dividends in your ability to tackle any plastic repair situation that comes along. Although the cost of the equipment up front is higher than with adhesives, the consumable ma-

Using a Molding Bar to Replace Broken Tabs

Some of the methacrylate adhesive kits on the market come with a *molding bar* which softens when heated and may be pressed over a pattern when softened to create a mold. Once cool, the mold is peeled off the pattern and attached to the area where the feature, such as a broken tab, needs to be restored. The mold is then filled with methacrylate adhesive.

In order for this to work, however, there must be an identical or similar feature on the part to use as a pattern. The following sequence shows how a tab on a street bike fairing might be restored using the molding bar. ■

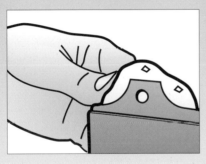

1. Place the molding bar in very hot water (near boiling) for two to three minutes until it softens.

2. Remove the molding bar from the water and immediately shape it over the pattern by hand. Press it around all the essential features (edges, holes, ridges, etc.) and maintain pressure until the bar cools and hardens. The cooling process can be expedited by running cool water over the molding bar.

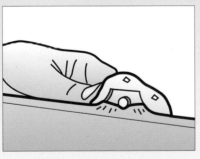

3. When the molding bar is completely cool, peel it from the pattern. The base material in the repair area should be sanded and tapered to maximize the surface area over which the adhesive may be applied. Place the molding bar in the area you want to restore the tab. It may need to be taped or clamped to hold it in the correct position.

4. Fill the mold with methacrylate adhesive using one of the application methods. Using this method, the new tab is *cast in place*, i.e., the tab is recreated and attached to the base material in one operation. Allow the adhesive plenty of time to cure (about one hour should be sufficient), then peel the molding bar away. The recreated tab will probably require some hand work with sandpaper or a die grinder to achieve its final shape. The molding bar is reusable. It may be heated again in hot water and shaped around another pattern.

Repairing Stripped Threads in Rigid Plastic
with Methacrylate Adhesive

Because methacrylate adhesive can duplicate very fine detail in a mold, it is ideal for use in restoring stripped threads in rigid, non-olefin plastics. In this case, the methacrylate adhesive is formed against the screw threads, which themselves act as a mold. The following sequence shows how screw threads can be restored. ■

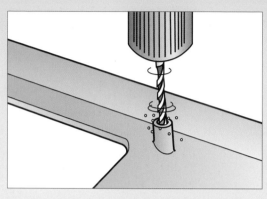

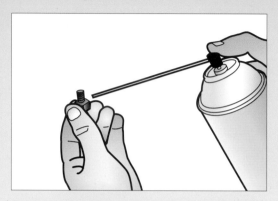

1. Drill out or file the stripped threads from the hole, allowing the screw to be slightly loose within it.

2. Apply lubricant liberally to the screw threads and to the bottom of the screw head. Motor oil, WD-40, Liquid Wrench, or petroleum jelly may be used. The oil will act as a mold release agent, allowing the screw to be unthreaded once the adhesive is cured.

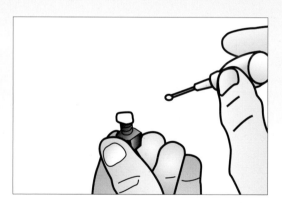

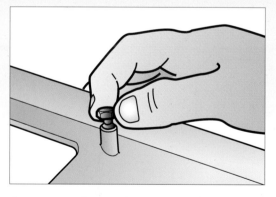

3. Using the mix method or the dropper method, apply methacrylate adhesive powder/liquid mixture directly to the screw threads. Apply enough to completely fill the cavity within the hole once the screw is inserted.

4. While the adhesive is wet, insert the screw into the hole. The excess adhesive should mushroom out. Wipe this excess adhesive off with a cloth. Allow the screw to sit in position for at least an hour and a half before attempting to unthread. When unthreaded, the screw will be tighter than the original because the female threads are molded hard up against the male threads, eliminating the clearance that is customary with standard thread design.

terial used in plastic welding is much less expensive, making welding more economical in the long run. In addition, with welding, there are no concerns with shelf life of the product as there often are with adhesives.

Properly done, a fusion weld on a thermoplastic can be stronger than an equivalent adhesive repair. The repair can be made even stronger if the heat of the welder is used to melt a stainless steel reinforcing wire mesh directly into the plastic substrate. In summary, having a plastic welder in your toolbox will allow you to make stronger, faster, less expensive repairs in many cases.

It does take a little more effort and practice to be able to reap these advantages, however. Whereas adhesives are often a "slap it on and walk away" proposition, welding requires a little more "face time" with the parts. You'll first have to identify the type of plastic and choose the appropriate filler rod. The welding process also takes more time than the simple act of applying an adhesive. Although the face time is greater, the total cycle time for making the repair is often a fraction that of an adhesive repair. Because the thermoplastic weld can be quenched with water immediately, a weld repair will attain its full strength in just a minute or two, while an adhesive repair often has to cure for an hour or more.

If you have decided that investing in a plastic welder makes sense for you, you'll have to decide between a hot-air welder and an airless welder. Hot-air welders have a much longer history than airless welders. Hot-air welders were originally and are still largely used to create fabrications from sheet stock and section. Fabrication work is characterized by the need to make long continuous welds over a consistent geometry. For example, if you were making a water storage tank from polyethylene sheet stock, you would cut rectangular pieces out and weld the sheets together at the corners. This process goes very quickly with a properly sized hot-air welder.

Repair work, on the other hand, is anything but consistent. The repair technician will be faced with a wide variety of plastic substrates, part geometries, and types of damage. Often, repairs have to be done in places where access is

limited. Airless welders tend to be better suited for such situations. They allow you to get into tighter spots, like the inside of a bumper cover, more easily. They allow physical contact with the substrate, enabling you to physically melt and mix the substrate with the filler rod. They also allow you to melt reinforcing mesh into the substrate, a technique that can't be done with a hot-air welder. Finally, with an airless welder, you can melt and apply hot-melt adhesives, which are useful for repairing TPO and thermoset urethanes.

Conversely, an airless welder would be painfully slow for doing long weld beads on a water storage tank, for example. So your choice of welder depends on the type of work you will do most often. Since you're reading this book, I assume you're more interested in repairing plastics than fabricating things from them. In that case, especially if you expect to be faced with a variety of plastics and parts, an airless welder may be better suited for you. However, if the only things you work on are dirt bike plastics, you might find it faster to use a hot-air welder.

Either way, in this section of the book I'll discuss how to perform fusion weld repairs with each type of welder—first the airless then the hot-air welder.

Fusion Welding with an Airless Plastic Welder

The word *fusion* itself distinguishes the process of welding from that of the use of adhesives. Whereas adhesives create a repair mainly by means of molecular attraction between dissimilar materials, the fusion welding process creates a repair by literally melting and mixing together the plastic of the substrate and filler rod. This process more or less creates a continuous, homogenous material in the weld zone.

Unfortunately, even if done perfectly, a weld will not have the same structural strength as the original material. The reason is that thermoplastics get their strength from the intermolecular attractive forces between long, randomly oriented polymer chains. When a plastic part is cracked, the polymer chains in the area are broken. If a weld is done, which fuses the substrate material with that of the filler rod, the outward appearance may be one of homogeneity, but at a molecular level, there will still be a discontinuity in the weld area. In other words, despite being welded, the polymer chains that had previously spanned over the crack are not restored to their original geometry. For this reason, unless the welded area is reinforced by some means, if the part is again subjected to destructive stress, particularly that which places the weld in tension, the part is likely to fail along the previously welded crack.

As I've stated before, this is not normally a problem because plastic parts usually break because they are subjected to an accidental destructive impact rather than a designed load. A welded repair, even unreinforced, will be more than strong enough to handle the stresses that would be expected in most cosmetic plastic parts. The only exception would be if the part were subjected to regular loads like an armrest or door handle. In such a case, a plastic weld will probably not be adequate without some additional reinforcement.

Creating a fusion weld with an airless plastic welder is simply a matter of using the welder to melt the filler rod together with the substrate. First, the temperature of the welding tip must be adjusted to suit the type of plastic that will be welded. For example, the melting point of nylon is much higher than that of ABS, so the temperature must accordingly be set higher if you want to weld nylon. Most airless plastic welders have a rheostat that controls the voltage and, thus, the temperature of the airless heating element.

Airless welders also require several minutes of start-up time before the heating element reaches the proper temperature. The heating element uses a nichrome wire coil wrapped around a steel core, insulated by mica. As current flows through the nichrome wire, the wire's natural electrical resistance causes it to heat up. This heat flows through the mica insulation into the steel core and welding tip. Allow five to seven minutes for the steel core and the welding tip to reach their steady state operating temperature.

Use the time that the welder is warming up to prepare your substrate for welding. The first step is, as always, clean and align the damaged area before starting your repair work. As with an adhesive repair, the crack must be V-grooved to ex-

pose more of the substrate's surface area for greater strength. In contrast with V-grooves for adhesive repairs, the V-groove doesn't need to be very wide (1/8 to 3/16 inch is sufficient) nor does it need to be sandscratched. If you can access both sides of the part, V-groove about halfway though the plastic on each side. If you cannot access the backside, like on a dirt bike gas tank or radiator tank, V-groove all the way through the plastic so the tip of the V-groove is at the inside surface of the tank.

There are two ways to create a V-groove in a thermoplastic. One way is to machine it in with a die grinder or sandpaper disc. In the case of welding, you don't have to be nearly as concerned with the surface finish as you have to be with adhesives. High-speed air tools may be used because it's not a problem if the substrate melts during the V-grooving process.

Another way to create the V-groove is to melt it into the plastic with a hot V-grooving tool. This may be a separate tool or a special tip that fits into the plastic welder's heating element. Melting the V-groove in simply displaces material outside of the V-groove, like the wake in front of a boat's prow. Leaving this material in place is an advantage if you want to build up the welded area higher than the surrounding surface for added strength. Conversely, if you are planning to grind the welded area flat and contour it, you may find it easier to machine in the V-groove as this permanently removes the excess material.

Before you feed the filler rod onto your repair, it is good practice to extrude an inch or two of welding rod onto a piece of scrap wood. This serves several purposes. First, the hole in the welder tip probably has burnt plastic inside from previous uses. Feeding a little rod through will help to clean the tip out and remove this blackened material. Second, feeding the rod through helps to stabilize the tip's temperature, which may have gotten too hot during the warm up process. Lastly, it gives you an opportunity to observe how well the rod melts as it comes through the feed tube and how fast it can be fed through while providing complete melting.

After you're comfortable with the element's temperature and the appearance of the melted

Fusion Welding With the Airless Plastic Welder

Most cracks in thermoplastics can be melted together again, or fusion welded. This process involves melting the base material together with a matching filler rod. Usually the most difficult part of the process is in identifying the plastic and selecting the proper filler rod. Once this is done, the repair process is as follows. ■

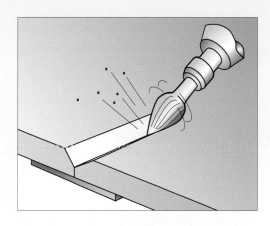

1. Align the frontside of the damaged area with aluminum body tape. Grind a narrow V-groove along the crack halfway through the plastic on the backside with a sharp pointed burr in a high-speed die grinder. The V-groove may also be melted into the plastic with a heated V-grooving tool. Grind off any paint in the surrounding area with coarse sandpaper and blow dust-free with compressed air.

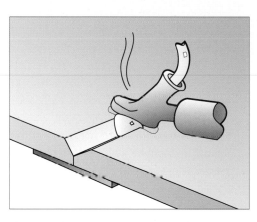

2. Lay the hot welder tip directly onto the surface of the plastic and make a slow pass along the crack, slowly feeding the filler rod through the welder tip. The filler rod should come out the bottom of the welder tip completely melted, but not scorched or smoking. Adjust welding temperature as necessary. Fill the V-groove for a length of about one inch, then stop and remove the filler rod from the welder tip.

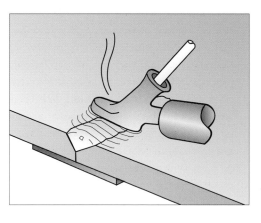

3. Go back over the filler rod you just applied and fuse together with the base material. Use the edge of the welder to mash across the crack, melting the base and filler rod, then mix the two materials and smooth out with the foot of the welder. Keep the heat on the area and continue to manually work the material until the base and filler rod are mixed to your satisfaction. Continue to add filler rod and mix in one-inch segments until the entire crack is fused together.

(cont. on next page)

Fusion Welding With the Airless Plastic Welder (Cont.)

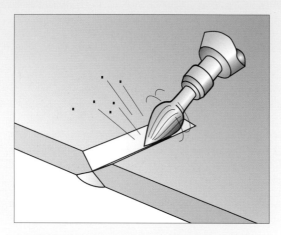

4. Allow the rod applied to the backside to cool completely, then peel off the tape on the frontside and V-groove halfway through the plastic on the frontside. Grind off any paint in the surrounding area with coarse sandpaper and blow dust-free with compressed air.

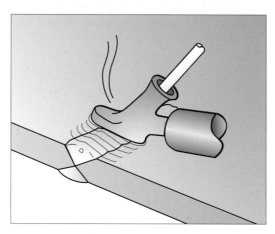

5. Repeat the welding process on the frontside. Melt filler rod into the V-groove in one-inch segments, then fuse completely with the base material by keeping the heat on it and manually working the base and filler rod together. Once the crack is completely welded and cooled, use a two-part filler to restore the cosmetic appearance of the frontside.

filler rod, immediately move to the repair area and, starting at one end of the V-groove, deposit a short ribbon of melted welding rod into the V-groove. Lay the welder's tip directly onto the substrate and slowly move the tip along as you feed the filler rod through the tip with your other hand. Keep a small, consistently sized bead of melted welding rod in front of the welder tip as you make your pass.

Lay your weld bead in short segments, about one to 1-1/2 inches long max. Welding in short segments allows the rod to maintain a high temperature, easing follow-on operations. Once you finish each segment, remove the filler rod from the feed tube and immediately go back over the welding rod you just applied with the hot welder tip. Use the welder tip to ensure that you have good fusion between the filler rod and the base. This can be done by mashing the sharp edge of the welder tip across the weld, then smoothing the displaced material back into the channel you created with the flat shoe of the welder tip. Once you're satisfied with the penetration of the weld, use the flat base of the tip to smooth out the surface. If the V-groove is very wide or deep, one pass with the welding rod may not be enough to fill up the V-groove. In such a case, immediately melt more rod into the V-groove along that segment to fill it up.

On plastics with higher melting points, like polycarbonate and nylon, the welding process can be accelerated by preheating the base material with a high-temp heat gun before you begin welding. This is a virtual necessity when welding a glass-reinforced nylon radiator tank. Preheat each segment that you plan to weld until the edges of the V-groove start to soften or appear glossy. Then immediately begin melting filler rod into the V-groove. Heating the base material first will greatly increase the ease with which the filler rod and the base material can be mixed together. Preheating is not usually required on plastics like ABS or polyethylene as their melting points are fairly low.

Radiator tanks present the most unforgiving plastic welding application because the high-pressure coolant in the tank will quickly find its way through any flaws in the weld. Therefore, proper fusion between the filler rod and base material is of the utmost importance. Fortunately, this is easy to verify visually because the filler rod is usually off-white in color, whereas the tank is usually black or dark brown. After you've preheated the area with a heat gun, melt the filler rod into the V-groove. There will be a ribbon of white rod surrounded by the black base material. Remove the welding rod from the tip and, using the techniques described above, melt the filler rod together with the surrounding base material until the whole area turns black or dark brown. Any white rod that remains visible indicates that you don't have sufficient penetration or fusion. Keep working the weld with the hot welder tip until all remaining traces of white filler rod disappear. This underscores the need to do your weld in short segments. If you get too ambitious and try to weld an entire four-inch-long crack in one pass, the plastic will cool down too much, making it more difficult to get proper penetration.

One thing to keep in mind is that the welder tip will cool down as you weld. Heat flows from hot objects to cooler ones, so as the heat flows into the plastic from the welder tip, the temperature of the welder tip will naturally go down. The nichrome coil in the element will be generating more heat to compensate, but it will probably not have the capacity to generate heat at the same rate that it's being withdrawn at the tip. Therefore, it will be necessary to occasionally stop welding for a minute or two to allow the welder to heat back up again. You will notice this when the welding rod does not come out quite as smoothly, or when you have to press the welder harder to move the plastic around. If that happens, take a short break and let the welder heat up again. Preheating the base material with a heat gun will also help the welder to stay hot longer because, by eliminating the requirement for the welder tip to heat up the substrate, heat is not being withdrawn from the welder tip at such a high rate.

Repeat the process of welding short segments of the weld until the entire crack has been welded. Allow 10 to 15 minutes for the plastic to cool, or, if you are in a hurry, quench the weld with cold water and compressed air. Once the weld on one side of the plastic has reached room temperature, the tape or clamps can be removed and the opposite side can be V-grooved and welded in the same manner.

An airless plastic welder is not only useful for fusion welding thermoplastics, but it can also be used to apply thermoplastic hot-melt adhesives to urethanes and TPOs. Because of its versatility, the airless plastic welder has a place in the toolbox of every person who plans to do more than just the occasional plastic repair.

Fusion Welding with a Hot-Air Welder

Hot-air welders are more difficult to use than airless welders, but in trained hands, they can work faster on certain plastics. As I mentioned before, hot-air welders are designed for fabrication work, but may be pressed into duty for repair work. Conversely, airless welders are designed for repair work, but are too slow to be considered for fabrication work. Because of their speed, many professional bumper recyclers use hot-air welders in their repair operations. Due to their difficulty of use, however, they aren't commonly used in body shops.

If you consistently do a lot of repair work on the same type of thermoplastic, a hot-air welder may be useful for you. An example would be a shop that specializes in doing street-bike fairing repair. Street-bike fairings are usually made of ABS and ABS/PC blends, which are easy to fusion weld with the hot-air welder. Plus, street bike fairings are easily removed and allow for clear access to both sides of the panel.

Bumper recycling shops that do repairs on lots of Honda bumpers, for example, can also make good use of the hot-air welder. Honda bumpers are TPO but have a low elastomer content, making them easy to weld with standard polypropylene filler rod. The greater the production level of a given shop, the more sense it makes to invest in a hot-air welder.

Although there are different designs, all hot-air welders work by the same basic principle. A controlled amount of air flows through an electric heating element and is directed through a nozzle onto the work area. The air may come from an internal blower or an external air compressor. The heating element may be metal or ceramic, but, in any case, it is designed like a heat

Fusion Welding a Plastic Radiator Tank

Nylon radiator tanks represent the most demanding plastic repair problem because any imperfections in the weld will become immediately obvious due to the pressure of the coolant behind it. Nylon also has one of the highest melting points of any plastic, so it takes more effort to obtain good fusion between the filler rod and base material. The following procedure can be used for parts where the backside of the material is not accessible. ■

1. Grind a V-groove along the crack all the way through the plastic with a sharp-pointed burr in a high-speed die grinder. The tip of the "V" should just begin to penetrate through to the backside of the tank.

2. Preheat a two-inch segment of the crack with a high-temp heat gun. Continue heating the area until the edges of the V-groove begin to soften or discolor slightly. This preheating process is not necessary on low temperature plastics like polyethylene.

3. Lay the hot welder tip directly onto the surface of the plastic and make a slow pass along the crack, slowly feeding the filler rod through the welder tip. The filler rod should come out the bottom of the welder tip completely melted, but not scorched or smoking. Adjust welding temperature as necessary. Fill the V-groove for a length of about one inch, then stop and remove the filler rod from the welder tip.

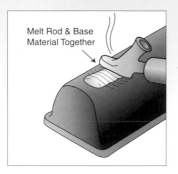

4. While it is still melted, go back over the filler rod you just applied and fuse together with the base material. Use the edge of the welder to mash across the crack, melting the base and filler rod, then mix the two materials and smooth out with the foot of the welder. On nylon, keep the heat on the area and continue to manually work the material until all traces of the white filler rod have turned dark brown or black. Continue to add filler rod and mix in one-inch segments until the entire crack is fused together.

exchanger, allowing the air passing by the element to heat up to the proper temperature.

Some hot-air welders offer a *speed tip* to help guide the rod and direct it properly into the stream of hot air, but most hot-air welders simply have a small round nozzle that expels a controlled amount of hot air, like a oxyacetylene welding torch. When using such a welder, the torch is held in one hand and the welding rod is fed with the other hand. The stream of hot air is directed onto the juncture between the rod and V-groove. Because of the coordination required by this process, it takes a bit of practice before it can be done well.

The flow rate of air from the welder tip must be carefully controlled. If too much air flows, there is a risk of blowing holes through the part you're trying to weld. Conversely, if not enough air flows, there is a risk of burning out the electric heating element inside the torch. It is also critical to turn off the electric heating element before turning off the flow of air. Often, if the air is turned off at the same time, the heating element will get too hot, causing an open circuit in the coil. Keeping a flow of air over the coil during the cool-down phase will vastly increase heating element life.

Preparation for a hot-air weld is the same as for airless plastic welding. Machine or melt in a V-groove halfway though the plastic or all the way through if the part is only accessible from one side, as on a fuel tank. On panels less than 3/16 inch thick, the V-groove should be about the width of the welding rod itself, often 1/8 inch. One pass with the welder on each side should be sufficient to fill the V-groove. If the substrate is especially thick or can only be accessed from one side, V-groove naturally at a 60-degree included angle and make several passes with the welder to fill the V-groove.

Just as on the airless welder, the heat setting for the hot-air welder must be set to the level appropriate for the type of plastic being welded. ABS plastics will melt too quickly if the temperature control is set too high, for example. Consult the chart for the melting temperatures for various types of plastics to get a feel for the appropriate temperature setting.

To begin the weld, direct the flow of hot air onto the beginning of the V-groove to begin melting the substrate. Lower the filler rod vertically at the same spot and direct hot air onto it as well to begin melting the bottom surface of the rod. Once the rod begins to soften, press down on it and begin to slowly feed the rod into the V-groove as you continuously direct the stream of hot air onto the juncture between the rod and base material. Using this process, a six-inch-long crack can be filled in just a matter of a minute. By contrast, an airless welder would require more than five minutes to do the same length of crack.

If you need to make more than one pass to fill up the V-groove, repeat the process immediately from the start of the V-groove again. In this case, the new filler rod will fuse with one side of the V-groove and the top of the first filler rod you laid in the groove.

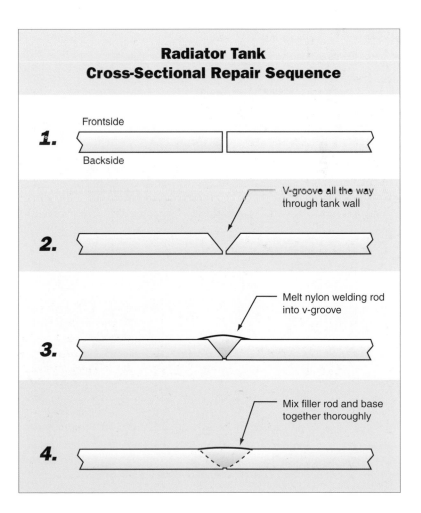

Radiator Tank Cross-Sectional Repair Sequence

1. Frontside
   Backside

2. V-groove all the way through tank wall

3. Melt nylon welding rod into v-groove

4. Mix filler rod and base together thoroughly

Care must be taken during the welding process to avoid warping the base material. The thinner the plastic, the more careful you must be. If the substrate is thinner than the filler rod, it is very difficult to do a proper weld without blowing though the substrate. On especially thin plastics, an airless welder is a better choice because it allows you to control heat input into the substrate more carefully.

The appearance of a hot-air weld will be much different than that of an airless weld. With the airless welder, the hot tool is in physical contact with the filler rod and substrate. The filler rod will be blended with the base material and smoothed out onto the surface. An airless weld will often look rough because the hot tip is used to mash into the plastic and mix the base with the filler rod.

Because there is no physical contact between the hot-air welder and the plastic substrate, the properly done hot-air weld will appear like the welding rod itself is laying in the V-groove. The unmelted or top surface of the welding rod will still have an unmolested, cylindrical appearance. The fusion has only taken place on the lower surface of the welding rod where it mates into the V-groove.

This characteristic gives hot-air welding its speed, because only the surfaces that will touch are melted and fused together. An airless welder has to melt the entire filler rod even though most of the melted rod will not be in direct contact with the base material. Also, an airless welder has to be run back over the weld to ensure proper fusion between the rod and base.

On the other hand, the fact that you can press directly on the plastic with airless welder has its advantages. First, it allows you to melt and apply hot-melt adhesives. Second, it allows you to press reinforcing mesh directly into the plastic. Neither of these useful operations can be done with a hot-air welder.

Solvent Welding

Solvent welding is a very convenient way of joining specific types of plastic, but it is much more commonly used for fabrication than repair work. In my seven years of experience in the field, I have never had the occasion to use a solvent weld in doing a repair. I present it here more for academic interest, so my coverage will be brief.

Solvent welds work by softening the surfaces to be joined with an appropriate solvent, then pressing the parts together. While they are softened, the molecules at the interface between the two parts will commingle, creating a good bond once the plastic hardens again.

Two things are essential for a good solvent welded joint. First, the parts must be lapped over one another. It is this factor that mainly limits the use of solvent welding for repair work. Most damage on plastics consists of cracks and holes. In such cases, plastic pieces come together at the crack in the form of a butt joint. To create a lap joint for a crack repair, you would have to make a tight-fitting backing patch that would lap over the crack on both sides.

Secondly, the parts must be pressed together or in close contact. This works beautifully for fabricating pipes where one pipe slides tightly within the other. It creates a problem for repair work as the geometry of most plastic parts is complicated. It is doubtful that you could find a

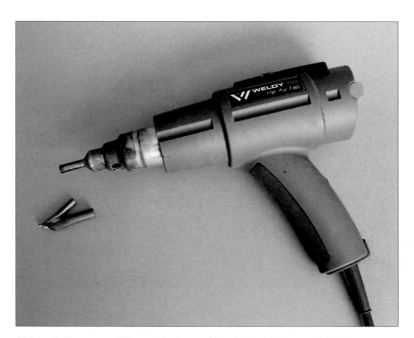

Although there are different designs, all hot-air welders work by the same basic principle: a controlled amount of air flows through an electric heating element and is directed through a nozzle onto the work area.

Fusion Welding with the Hot-Air Welder

Fusion welding with a hot-air welder can be much faster than with an airless plastic welder as long as the geometry of the damage and the part itself allows its use. Hot-air welding is a two-handed method that requires more physical space and more skill and coordination to perform. ■

1. Align the frontside of the damaged area with aluminum body tape. Grind a narrow V-groove along the crack halfway through the plastic on the backside with a sharp pointed burr in a high-speed die grinder. The V-groove may also be melted into the plastic with a heated V-grooving tool. Grind off any paint in the surrounding area with coarse sandpaper and blow dust-free with compressed air.

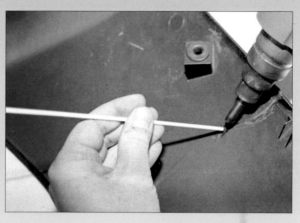

2. Starting at one end of the crack, direct the stream of hot air onto the V-groove and tip of the rod until both begin to soften. The base material will require more heat input than the filler rod to achieve the same temperature.

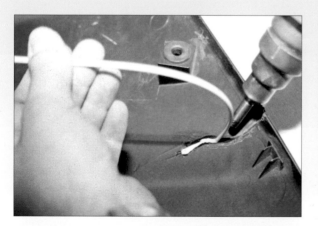

3. Press down on the rod in such a way that it curves in toward and lays inside the V-groove. Slowly lay the rod in the V-groove while moving the stream of hot air to soften the base material and rod just ahead of the point where they touch. Make sure the base material and rod are thoroughly softened before they come together.

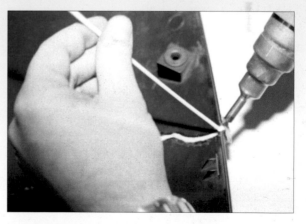

4. Continue feeding the rod in this manner until the V-groove is filled with the welding rod. Because the weld cannot be physically worked as it can be in airless welding, you will see the welding rod's round profile in the top of the V-groove. On either side of the round profile of the rod you should see a distorted area where the rod and base material are melted together.

backing patch that would follow all of the contours of the part along the entire length of the crack.

PVC and ABS are two common plastics that can be solvent welded. To do so, simply clean the surfaces in the areas to be joined. A light sandscratch in the area might be desirable to get deeper penetration of the solvent into the plastic, but it is not necessary. Using a PVC or ABS cement commonly available in the plumbing section of any hardware store, brush the solvent onto both surfaces to be joined. Press them together immediately and clamp if necessary. After some amount of time, the softened plastic surfaces will join together as one. Wait the recommended amount of time before applying any load to the freshly welded joint.

Refinishing Plastics

Unless the part you've repaired is hidden under the hood or behind a fairing, you are probably interested in refinishing or painting the part to restore its original appearance. Most of the high-dollar plastic parts that you're likely interested in repairing are cosmetic, painted components like bumper covers and street-bike fairings. These parts will have to be refinished before the repair can be considered complete.

Before applying primer and paint to a repaired part, it is critically important to have a smooth surface over the repair area with an undetectable transition from the substrate to the filler. There are two steps to this process. The first, and easiest, is applying a two-part filler over the repair area as per Chapter 4. The second and more time-consuming step is the use of lots of elbow grease. Block sanding the damaged area by hand using progressively finer grits of sandpaper is the best way to get the profile correct before you apply the primer. Skilled body technicians can accelerate this process with the use of air-powered sanders, but such tools can be dangerous in the hands of the unskilled person. Be patient, take it slow and easy, and get the profile right before you spray on the primer.

Once you get the profile of the surface over the repair area acceptably smooth to the eye and hand, you are ready to begin the refinishing process. From this point on, the process followed for refinishing depends on the type of plastic from which the substrate is made. All plastics fall into one of several categories with regard to the ease with which they can be repaired. I'll discuss the specifics for each of these categories in this chapter.

There are five categories of refinishing procedures based on the type or characteristics of the plastic. In order of increasing difficulty, they are:

- Rigid, non-olefin plastics (thermoset and thermoplastic)
- Flexible, non-olefin plastics (mainly thermoset polyurethane)
- TPO and PP, painted
- TPO and PP, unpainted, textured
- Polyethylene

Most plastics on cars and motorcycles, like ABS, GTX, polycarbonate, fiberglass, and SMC, will fall into the first category. These plastics are very easy to refinish as the primer coat

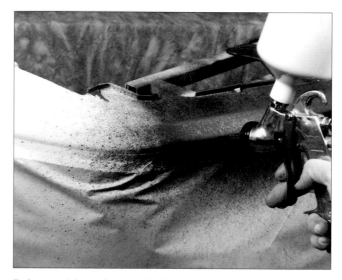

Before applying primer and paint to a repaired part, it is critically important to have a smooth surface over the repair area with an undetectable transition from the filler to the substrate.

will have good adhesion to the substrate. Primers also have good adhesion to flexible thermoset polyurethanes. These are made only slightly more difficult as the refinishing materials must also be flexible.

The real problems arise on the olefin plastics, like PP, TPO, and PE. Painted TPOs are fairly easy to refinish as long as the proper adhesion promoter is used prior to application of the first primer coat. Unpainted, textured TPOs are much more difficult to repair and require special preparation and refinishing techniques to simulate the original appearance. Finally, polyethylene is so difficult to get adhesion to that it is almost not worth trying.

No matter what the substrate is made of, if the original part is painted and the paint still intact and has good adhesion to the substrate, then it is best to leave the original finish in place and refinish over the top of it. Removing all of the original paint is usually too time consuming and risks damaging the base material further through the use of paint strippers or abrasives. This is especially true on TPO parts. Aftermarket primer is not likely to have the same level of adhesion to the substrate as the OEM applied primer.

If the paint on the part is cracked or damaged over a large area, or especially if it is brittle due to long exposure to the elements, it may not be worth trying to repair the part in the first place. Refinishing a large plastic part is usually the most time-consuming step of the total repair process, so tackling a part with lots of paint cracks and chips is going to greatly increase the total time required to finish the job. This factor should have been taken into account during the decision to repair or replace, covered in Chapter 1.

In situations where you have done a spot repair on a plastic part, you usually only have to expose the raw plastic in the area immediately around the repair. Assuming the original paint is otherwise in good condition, the refinishing operation will be about the same for any type of plastic substrate. The only consideration would be to the proper adhesion promoters on any exposed raw plastic areas on TPO prior to application of the primer surfacer.

If the damage is confined to a small area, you may feel comfortable in spot refinishing and

blending. In this case, you'd simply apply the color coat only to the repair area, not to the entire part. Blending the color and the clearcoat with the original finish requires some experience to do properly, however. If you don't have experience in blending, it would probably be easier to refinish the entire part. For the purposes of this book, I'll assume you're going to be refinishing the entire part, not blending.

If the part is decorated with stick-on decals, as many motorcycle sidecovers are, they will have to be removed before doing an overall refinish. They are more easily peeled up after softening the adhesive with a heat gun. Remove the tacky adhesive remnants with a plastic cleaning solvent. If you would prefer to save the decals, try doing a spot repair and mask off the decals.

I'll start with an exhaustive description of how to refinish rigid, non-olefin plastics, and then describe the special procedures that should be followed when refinishing other types of plastics.

Refinishing Rigid, Non-Olefin Plastics

Assuming that the repair you made using the procedures detailed in Chapter 4 is smoothed out with an even transition (featheredge) to the part's original surface, you are ready to begin the refinishing procedure. Again, I'll assume that you'll be refinishing the entire panel, not blending. That being the case, since you're going to be applying primer to the entire part, you're going to have to prepare the entire part for application of the primer coat.

If you didn't clean the entire part before doing the repair, it's time to do it now. Avoid wetting the repair area, but clean the entire surface to be painted with soap and water, then a plastic cleaning solution. Again, it's always best to clean the entire part before beginning the repair process, but sometimes people shortcut the procedures and only clean the repair area at first. It's better to clean the rest of the part after the fact than not to do it at all.

Before moving on, closely inspect the condition of the surface you are planning to paint. First of all, is it painted, or is it raw plastic? Most thermoset rigid plastics, like SMC or fiberglass, will be painted or at least have a gel coat. Most decorative automotive and motorcycle rigid thermoplastic panels will also be painted. If the part is painted, the color of the outer surface of the part will be different from the color of the base material of the plastic. You can tell this by observing the featheredge around the repair area. If the part is painted, there should be a halo around the repair area showing the transition from paint to primer to base material.

If the part is painted, is the paint in good condition? If it is cracked all over, dry rotted, or if there are chunks falling off, you must sand all the paint off down to the base material and start from scratch.

Second, is there already another refinish coat on the part? You can determine this by again looking at the featheredge around the repair area. If the outer color coat transitions to a primer color and then back to a color again, then the part has been refinished once already. Many times, the adhesion of refinish coats is not to the same standard as the original OEM finish. Rather than take a chance with the quality of the previous refinish job, it is best to strip off or sand off the refinish coat first. Leave the OEM finish intact and begin your refinishing process by priming on top of that.

Finally, is the surface glossy? Whether the surface is painted or not, primer will not stick to a glossy surface. A glossy surface is to adhesion as rat poison is to a rat—it kills. The entire surface of the part to be painted must be sanded with 320-grit sandpaper to remove the gloss. That includes all the corners and trim lines where it's hard to get a piece of sandpaper into. Again, as long as the original paint is in good condition, there's no need to sand it all off. You just need to put some fine sandscratches into the surface to maximize the surface area over which the paint will adhere. A sandblaster is helpful to get into all the nooks and crannies where it's impossible to get with sandpaper. If you use a sandblaster, be careful and go lightly. You just need to knock off the shine, not remove the paint completely.

If you used a plastic prep soap to clean the surface, there may be some surface scratch to help with the adhesion, but it probably won't be quite enough. Again, if you see any shiny spots between the sandscratches, keep sanding. Surface preparation is the most important part of getting a durable refinish job. Unfortunately, it's a time consuming, tedious job—one that you may be tempted to shortcut. If you want a durable, high-quality refinish job, resist the temptation and keep sanding!

Once you've got the surface properly sanded, blow the dust off with clean, dry compressed air, or wipe it off with a clean cloth. Compressed air is preferable as it can blow small particles out of the sandscratches that the cloth won't touch. However, if the air is wet or, even worse, oily, it would be best not to use the air at all. From this

Refinishing Process Flowchart

Sand surface smooth and feather repair areas out with 180 to 320 grit sandpaper, depending on substrate. Remove gloss from entire area to be refinished with 320 grit sandpaper. Pay special attention to hard-to-reach areas around trim, edges, and corners. Blow dust free.

↓

If substrate is TPO, spray adhesion promoter on raw plastic areas.

↓

Apply two medium coats of (flexible) primer surfacer.

↓

Sand primer surfacer with 320 or 400 grit paper, fill any remaining imperfections with spot putty or catalyzed filler. Sand again with 400 grit paper.

↓

If substrate is TPO, spray adhesion promoter on any raw plastic areas that may have broken through.

↓

Apply one medium coat of (flexible) primer surfacer. Sand with 400 grit paper. If any imperfections remain, repeat filling and sanding process.

↓

Apply (flexible) sealer coat if necessary.

↓

Apply desired color coat system. Add flex additive if necessary.

Refinishing Non-Olefin Plastics

Refinishing rigid, non-olefin plastics is the most straightforward of all plastic refinishing processes. Refinishing flexible, non-olefin plastics is identical except that you will need to use a flexible primer surfacer and add flex additive to the color coat to maintain paint film flexibility. The following is a generic description of the refinishing process; if the directions for the specific refinishing product you are using differs, use them instead. ■

1. Sand the surface to be refinished with 180- to 320-grit sandpaper in a DA sander. Depending on the primer, 180 may be too coarse, or 320 too fine. 220-grit is often a good compromise. Blow dust-free with clean, dry, compressed air.

2. Apply primer surfacer to the part. Unless the part is very rigid, like SMC or Xenoy, use a flexible primer surfacer. Follow product instructions, but it is usually recommended to apply in two medium coats, allowing 5 to 15 minutes of flash time between coats. Allow primer to dry completely.

3. Block sand primer with 400-grit sandpaper, wet or dry. Blow dust-free and use tack rag to remove remaining dust particles.

4. Apply color coat per product instructions. For base-clear systems, spray only enough base coat to hide underlying color differentials and achieve uniform appearance. Depending on the rigidity of the substrate, you may choose to add a flex additive to the paint. For base-clear refinishing systems, flex additive is not needed in the base, only the clear.

point on, you need to be very careful not to get any oil on the part. That means keep your hands clean (use latex gloves if possible) and save the pizza until you're finished with the job.

Let's say you've got the surface of the part completely sanded to a dull finish with the sanding dust removed. You are finally ready to shoot some primer. Which primer, you ask? First of all, since you're doing a repair, you'll probably have some minor surface imperfections that you'll need to sand out before applying a color coat. Therefore, the primer should be easily sandable and should have a fairly high build to allow it to fill in those small imperfections. A *primer surfacer* or a *sandable primer* is what you need. If the plastic is rigid, there is no need to buy a special flexible primer intended for use on flexible plastics. A primer intended for use on metal may also be used.

There are a wide variety of primer surfacers available, from spray cans you can buy at the local hardware store to two-part epoxy systems. If you are a do-it-yourselfer, go with the spray can. To use anything more serious is going to require an air compressor and spray gun. If you have this equipment already, visit your local autobody supply store. These stores usually cater to the professional, but they'll sell to do-it-yourselfers in most areas. For rigid, non-olefin plastics, any primer surfacer will work. One-part lacquer-based primers are the least expensive, they dry quickly, and they are easy to use. Two-part epoxy or urethane primers will provide better adhesion and impact resistance, but they will be more expensive and more complicated to use. Use the best paint system you can afford and feel comfortable using, however, for the do-it-yourselfer, a good quality one-part lacquer primer should provide excellent results. Keep in mind that the primer should be compatible with the color coat system you plan to use. Thoroughly read the application instructions of your color coat system before purchasing primer.

Mix and apply the primer according to the product instructions. The primer will usually be applied in two medium coats with some *flash* time between coats. Flash time refers to the time required for the excess solvents to evaporate. The resins and fillers in the primer surfacer are blended with solvents to allow them to be sprayed onto a surface. Once a thin film of wet paint is applied, the solvents will begin to evaporate from the paint film, leaving behind the resins and fillers. Most paint systems will require at least a partial evaporation of the solvents before applying a second coat. Also, it is better to apply two medium coats than one single heavy coat because it may be difficult for all the solvents to evaporate from a thicker paint film. If subsequent paint coats trap solvents underneath, they will eventually evaporate and cause the paint to bubble up. Follow the procedures recommended by the manufacturer of the product to avoid any such mishaps.

After the primer surfacer has dried (or cured, if it's a two-part system), block sand the entire surface again with 320-grit paper. You may choose to wet sand the primer, which will help to keep the sandpaper clear and the surface smooth and free from dust. Once the primer is sanded and dried, look closely for any remaining minor imperfections, like heavy sandscratches, pinholes, and the like. Fill these imperfections with a one-part lacquer glazing putty and sand again. Don't use a glazing putty for anything deeper or larger than 1/32 inch. If you have any defects larger than this, use a thermosetting epoxy or polyester filler to fill them.

Prime and sand again, and repeat the process as necessary until the surface finish reaches your expectations. The final coat of primer should be sanded with 400-grit sandpaper. Don't break through the primer to expose any raw plastic on your final sanding step. For the most uniform appearance, the color coat should be applied over a consistent coat of primer.

Before spraying on the color, most paint systems recommend the use of a sealer coat between the primer surfacer and the color. The sealer provides a barrier so that the solvents in the color coat system do not attack underlying coatings and repair materials. Often, a sealer coat is unnecessary, but to be safe, closely follow the instructions provided by the color coat manufacturer.

As for the color coat, there are a number of ways you can go depending on the equipment you have and your expectations of the finished surface's appearance and durability. In terms of increasing cost (and quality), the options for color coats are as follows:

- Aerosol spray can, enamel paint
- Acrylic lacquer
- Acrylic enamel or urethane, single stage
- Acrylic urethane, base-clear system (two-stage)

For the most professional finished appearance, either a urethane base-clear or a single-stage system should be used. These are available at any autobody supply store. They are expensive, but worth it in terms of coating durability and appearance. The coatings go on wet and flow out to give a smooth glossy appearance without time-consuming wet sanding and polishing. Base-clear systems especially have excellent resistance to attack from gasoline and other solvents, so they make the best choice for motorcycle tanks. They can also be mixed to match the exact color that you need.

There are a couple of drawbacks to urethane, especially base-clear systems, with regard to the do-it-yourselfer. First, the coatings stay tacky for a while after they are applied, so they tend to attract dust and bugs. The overspray also remains tacky and will stick to and possibly ruin any thing else that's sitting in the area. These are not usually problems in a professional body shop where such coatings are sprayed in a filtered paint booth. But they can be a big problem if you're spraying in your garage or, worse yet, outdoors.

Second, these paints are catalyzed with chemicals containing *isocyanates, which are nasty and harmful if breathed in.* If you don't have proper respiratory protection equipment, don't even think about spraying catalyzed urethane paint.

Acrylic lacquer paints are a good option for the do-it-yourselfer. They can be custom mixed to match the original paint, they aren't nearly as hazardous as catalyzed urethanes, and the overspray is usually dry before it hits the ground.

Unfortunately, to get a glossy finish, lacquers have to be wet sanded and polished, so it takes a lot of effort to get it looking good. Furthermore, their long-term durability is not up to the standards of a catalyzed urethane paint. Lacquer also cannot withstand repeated exposure to gasoline. Finally, because acrylic lacquers are rarely used in body shops today, they can be difficult to find.

You probably wouldn't consider refinishing a glossy, Class A automotive or motorcycle exterior part with an aerosol can of enamel paint, but they can come in handy for painting trim items like door handles and rub strips. The biggest advantage of spray cans is their convenience; most importantly, no air compressor or paint gun is required. But you pay for that convenience with degraded appearance and durability of the coating. Uncatalyzed enamel paints are a poor choice in an area where they may be exposed to gasoline.

Whichever system you choose, if you're painting on a rigid plastic with a properly prepared primer coat, simply mix the paint and apply it according to product instructions. There is no need for a flex additive in the paint when applied to rigid plastics. In this sense, the paint can be applied just as it would be applied to a steel substrate.

If you choose to apply heat to the part to speed the cure rate of the paint film, use only medium- or long-wave infrared (IR) light. Some newer lights use *short-wave* IR technology. Short-wave light is intended for use on steel panels. The IR light passes right through the paint film, heats the metal, and heats the paint from the inside out. However, because plastic substrates cannot dissipate heat like steel panels can, short-wave IR can overheat plastics very quickly. Also, when using medium- or long-wave IR light, hold the light back farther and don't allow the panel temperature to exceed 140 degrees F. If you overheat the part, you may damage the underlying repair material or warp the part itself. When in doubt, be patient and don't heat the part.

Refinishing Flexible, Non-Olefin Plastics

There's a gray area between the definition of a flexible plastic and a rigid one, at which point you'll have to use some judgment. The most flexible, non-olefin plastic is the thermoset polyurethane commonly used on bumper covers.

These can be flexed over a small radius, on the order of three to six inches. On the other end of the scale, you've got rigid plastics like SMC and Xenoy, which, if molded in the form of a bumper or reinforcement, can't be flexed even the slightest amount.

Part geometry plays a big role in the rigidity of the part. Even Xenoy, if molded in a plain sheet, can be flexed over a six- to twelve-inch radius. But most rigid plastics, certainly those injection-molded parts suitable for automotive or motorcycle use, have a variety of surfaces and features at different angles to one another that serve to make the part difficult to bend (i.e., features that increase the sectional modulus of the part, in engineering terms).

If the part can be flexed any appreciable amount using your bare hands, it would be wise to assume that the part is *flexible,* although it might be more properly classified as semi-rigid or semi-flexible. The point is that if the part itself is flexible, the primer and paint coatings that are applied to it must also be flexible. If they are not and the part is flexed, the paint may crack. However, if you use a flexible primer and paint on a rigid plastic, no problem. Therefore, it's safer to err on the side of using a flexible paint system if there's any doubt.

Flexible, non-olefin plastics can be repaired using the same basic procedure as rigid, non-olefin plastics, the only exception being that the primer and paint used should remain flexible after they dry. Most automotive-grade paints and primers can be *flexiblized* with the use of a flex additive. Flexible primers and paints can also be purchased that are ready to spray, some even in aerosol cans. Such specialty products are not available at the local hardware store; you'll have to purchase these products at an autobody supply store.

The best policy for buying a flexible paint system (or any paint system, for that matter) is to work backward from the finish coat. Select the type of finish coat you want to use (base-clear, single-stage, lacquer), then buy whatever flex additive you need to make the finish coat flexible. Then purchase the recommended sealer and primer surfacer, with flex additive, if necessary. This way you'll have complementary products

all the way through from beginning to end. The only problem is that the cost of your purchase can get into significant triple digits very quickly!

There are several companies that produce aftermarket paint and coatings that can save you a significant amount of money. Most of these companies make undercoats (primers) and/or clears, leaving the color basecoats to the major manufacturers like DuPont and PPG. There are even a couple of companies that offer alternatives to the majors in the color basecoat department. These aftermarket companies all claim compatibility with the products of other companies. Choosing this route takes more experience, however. If you are a do-it-yourselfer doing such refinishing for the first time, it would be advisable to stick with the products of one manufacturer throughout to ensure compatibility.

Refinishing Painted TPO and PP Substrates

TPO and PP are members of a family of plastics called *olefins.* These plastics naturally have a very low surface energy, making it difficult for paints and adhesives to stick to them. Paint can and will stick sufficiently well to them, but great care must be taken to clean the part and to prepare its surface properly before applying the first coat of primer.

I have separated the refinishing process of painted and unpainted TPOs for a reason: as long as the original paint is not cracked or otherwise damaged over a large area and has good adhesion to the substrate, painted TPOs are much easier to refinish. Just sand the original paint and apply the primer on top of the original paint. In essence, the majority of the surface to be refinished will be a thermoset urethane plastic paint film, not TPO plastic. Primer will have good adhesion to the existing paint film. The only areas of raw plastic that will need to be coated will be in the repair area where the original paint was sanded off.

If the paint is flaking off, chipped, cracked, or otherwise damaged over a large area, it will be necessary to strip the original finish off to the raw plastic. The safest way to do this is to sand it off by hand. As you can imagine, this is a very time-consuming and physically tiring job. Before going to such lengths, reevaluate your decision to repair and refinish the part versus simply replacing the part with a new one. TPO plastics tend to be less expensive. If, however, the part is rare or unavailable, you may not have a choice but to strip the paint off and refinish from scratch.

To refinish TPO plastic, use the same procedures as are used on flexible, non-olefin plastics. The only exception would be the requirement for an *adhesion promoter* or *surface modifier* over any raw plastic areas prior to the application of the first coat of primer. There are some flexible primer surfacers that do not require an adhesion promoter over TPO; check the application instructions on your specific product. I can only give general guidelines for the refinishing process in this book; the product instructions trump any rules of thumb stated here.

It's a good idea to apply a spot of primer surfacer over the repair area at first before priming overall. This will help to replace the paint film that was sanded off during the repair process, getting the surface up to the same level. Block sand the area with 320-grit paper and feather the primer surfacer out onto the paint. More than one application of primer surfacer may be required to level out the surface.

This process is especially important on film-coated TPO plastics. Film-coating is a relatively new process that is sure to grow in the first decade of the twenty-first century. When the part is manufactured, instead of being spray painted, a sheet of colored film is placed in the mold and the plastic is injected in behind the paint film. Film coated parts can be distinguished by the lack of paint overspray on the edges or backside. Usually, the paint film will end at a sharp line.

The problem with refinishing such parts is that the clearcoat film layer does not feather out well on the underlying color coat film layer. Surrounding the repair area will be a halo defined by the coarse edge of the clearcoat film. The only way to finish this out is to build up the repair area and outside the halo with primer surfacer, then block sand back to a smooth contour that is slightly higher than the original surface. This way, the coarse edge of the clearcoat film is buried beneath the layer of primer surfacer.

Once the repair areas are leveled out to your satisfaction, apply an overall coat of flexible primer to the part. Again, first spray adhesion promoter to any raw plastic areas that were exposed during the preparation process. After the primer dries, block sand the entire part with 320- or 400-grit and check closely for any imperfections. Fill any imperfections with a flexible spot putty or flexible glaze, sand, and repeat the priming process. Repeat until you are satisfied with the appearance of the surface. The final primer coat should be sanded with 400-grit paper. The color coat can then be applied as it would be for a non-olefin flexible plastic.

Refinishing Unpainted TPO and PP Substrates

Unpainted TPO plastics present the most challenging problem in the area of plastic parts refinishing. In addition to the fact that TPOs are inherently difficult to gain adhesion to, most such TPOs have a surface texture molded directly into the cosmetic surface of the part that must also be restored or simulated. Most have a small *pebble grain* that may be simulated with a texture spray. However, some, like the Pontiac Aztek and Chevrolet Avalanche, have a specific geometric pattern embossed in the surface that, to this point, have defied any attempts at simulation.

If you see a regular geometric pattern molded into the surface of the plastic when you look closely at it, throw the part away and buy a new one. As of this writing, there is no technology that will allow you to restore such surface detail on a TPO substrate. If the part is irreplaceable or very expensive, you may consider sanding off all the texture and retexturing with a texture spray. The part won't match the original, but at least it gives you an option for repairing the original part.

As is so often the case, your (or your customer's) expectations for the appearance of the repair will drive the decision. If the vehicle is only one year old and an insurance company is paying for the damage, the only choice will be to replace the damaged part with a new one. However, if it's your own 9-year-old vehicle and you're paying for the repairs out of your own

Refinishing Painted TPO Plastics

Refinishing painted TPO parts is similar to refinishing flexible non-olefin parts except that adhesion promoters should be used and special care should be taken to keep from fuzzing up the substrate before applying primer. ■

1. Sand the surface to be refinished with 220- and 320-grit sandpaper at slow speed in a DA sander. Although it is considered too fine for most primers, it is usually best to sand with 320-grit on TPOs. TPOs have a tendency to get fuzzy if too coarse a sandpaper is used. 320-grit will knock down the fuzz and prevent it from poking up above the primer coat. Blow dust-free with clean, dry, compressed air.

2. Follow product instructions, but most primer surfacers require the use of an adhesion promoter when applied to raw TPO. Spray the adhesion promoter overall, or just on the raw TPO exposed by the sanding process. Allow the solvents in the adhesion promoter to evaporate per product instructions.

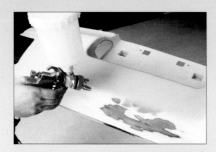

4. Apply flexible primer surfacer to the part. Follow product instructions, but it is usually recommended to apply in two medium coats, allowing 5 to 15 minutes of flash time between coats. Allow primer to dry completely.

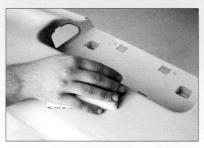

3. Block sand primer with 400-grit sandpaper, wet or dry. Blow dust-free and use tack rag to remove remaining dust particles.

5. Apply color coat per product instructions. For base-clear systems, spray only enough base coat to hide underlying color differentials and achieve uniform appearance. Depending on the rigidity of the substrate, you may choose to add a flex additive to the paint. For base-clear refinishing systems, flex additive is not needed in the base, only the clear.

Refinishing Unpainted, Textured TPO Plastics

Refinishing unpainted, textured TPO parts is the most difficult task in the realm of plastic refinishing. The original, stippled texture cannot be duplicated, only *simulated* using a special texture spray. This texture is difficult to blend; it is often better to sand off the texture completely, then refinish. Care must be taken to keep from scarring the soft plastic with coarse sandpaper before applying primer. ■

1. Sand the surface to be retextured with 320-grit sandpaper at slow speed in a DA sander. If you decide to remove existing texture completely, begin with 180-grit, then finish sand with 220 and 320. If you decide to blend the texture, keep the sanded area to a minimum. Blow dust-free with clean, dry, compressed air.

2. Spray adhesion promoter on the area to be retextured. Allow the solvents in the adhesion promoter to evaporate per product instructions.

3. Apply flexible texture material to the part. Adjust air pressure, fluid flow, and distance to work to vary the appearance of the sprayed-on texture. A lower air pressure will result in a larger grain. Apply several light coats until you achieve an appearance that is acceptable. After texture material dries, scuff lightly with a scuff pad to remove dry spray and to help blend in with the original texture.

4. Apply final color coat per product instructions. Use a thin, single-stage color coat with appropriate satin appearance when dry. It may be preferable to color coat entire part rather than attempt to blend.

pocket, sanding all the texture off may be a perfectly acceptable alternative.

If the part has a pebbled grain pattern that looks random from a short distance, there's a good chance that you'll be able to restore the appearance of the part to an acceptable level using a texture spray. The texture spray is typically a lacquer-borne primer that goes on a little "lumpy." Adjusting the fluid flow and air pressure at the paint gun, among other things, can vary the size and appearance of the lumps in the texture. With a little practice, you can closely simulate the appearance of the texture in the plastic.

However, retexturing a plastic part is more art than science. Even people with experience may sometimes only produce mediocre results. For this reason, think hard about the possibility of replacing the part rather than repairing and refinishing it. The cost of textured TPO plastics are usually at the lower end of the scale, so it often doesn't make sense to repair such parts, especially when you consider that refinishing them can be so problematic.

If you decide that a repair must be done, here's how to do it. Clean the plastic thoroughly using the procedures described in Chapter 4. If you are planning to refinish the entire panel, it is best to use a plastic prep soap with a soft cloth. The abrasives in the soap with put a very fine, almost invisible, sandscratch into the plastic that will help the paint to stick.

When you do the repair, be very careful not to sand the plastic with anything coarser than 180-grit. It is practically impossible to hide deep sandscratches in the soft, textured TPO. Keep the repair area restrained to the smallest possible area to minimize the amount of retexturing that must be done.

If there is a natural break, like a trim line, in the part, your job will be much easier if you sand off all the texture in the area up to the break line then retexture the entire area. Blending the retexture spray into the original texture is much more difficult to do.

Sand the texture off and with 180-grit, then smooth out the plastic with 220- and 320-grit. This is normally not recommended because 320-grit is a bit too fine to get a sandscratch that is good for adhesion. However, on unpainted TPO, an exception must be made because the TPO tends to "fuzz up" when sanded with anything coarser than 320-grit. These fuzzies will stick up out of the paint and cause the repair area to be easily visible.

When the area to be retextured is completely smoothed out with 320-grit, spray on a coat of adhesion promoter following the product instructions. This will help the texture material to get a good grip on the substrate.

Before spraying on the texture material, practice spraying on a test panel or scrap piece of plastic to get a feel of how the paint goes on. Spray the texture on in several light coats. If you use heavy coats, the paint will flow out and ruin the pebbled appearance you are trying to achieve. Variables you can adjust include the fan size, fluid flow, distance from work surface, and air pressure. Lowering the air pressure will give a coarser grain; increasing it will yield a finer grain. Experiment with the variables until you get a texture size that closely resembles the original, then spray the texture on the part to be repaired.

After the texture material has dried, lightly rub over the area with a fine scuff pad to blend the spray texture with the original and to remove any dry spray. Blow the area dust-free with clean, dry, compressed air. If you are not satisfied with the appearance of the texture at this point, sand it back off with 320-grit paper and start over. It may be hard to see how the texture will look until it is color coated, however.

The final step is to color coat the repair area or entire part. Select a paint that is designed for textured bumper refinishing or have a matching color custom mixed at your local autobody supply store. Use a lacquer or urethane single-stage product, not a base-clear system. The gloss should be low or satin to match the original. If you use a custom-mixed product, slightly over-reduce it to thin it out. The paint should be very thin to keep it from flowing out and filling up the texture.

The color coat you choose may or may not require an adhesion promoter prior to application. Follow the instructions for your product. If it is required, apply the adhesion promoter, wait the prescribed amount of time, then apply two light coats of paint. First, apply paint over the repair area to confirm that its appearance is acceptable. If not, you will need to sand off the texture and start over again, so it's best to not refinish the entire part until you know you're satisfied with the appearance of the repair area. If so, continue the process and apply paint to the entire part.

As you can see from this description, refinishing textured, unpainted TPO parts is fraught with difficulty, especially for the novice. Be sure to keep these factors in mind when you're deciding whether to go through with a repair or not.

Refinishing Polyethylene Substrates

Polyethylene is most commonly used on applications like radiator overflow bottles or washer fluid tanks, underhood parts where the function of the part is far more important than its appearance. These parts are easily recognizable because they are molded in polyethylene's trademark milky-white, slightly translucent natural color.

One of the few applications where polyethylene parts must also serve a cosmetic function is on dirt bike and ATV fenders. Polyethylene's trademark semi-translucent appearance is maintained, but these parts are molded in color—Honda red, Kawasaki green, etc.—and are characterized by their flexibility and their slick, almost oily surface.

Because of its toughness and low cost, polyethylene is an excellent choice of material for dirt bike and ATV fenders. Furthermore, polyethylene's naturally oily nature makes it hard for mud and dirt to stick to it and easy to clean.

Unfortunately, these characteristics also make it hard for repair materials and paint to stick to it. As I have mentioned, polyethylene is virtually impossible for adhesives to stick to, so welding is the only viable, long-term repair option. Even if the part is welded, it can't be restored to its pre-accident condition because the weld can't be smoothed out with putty or painted.

Therefore, if you want the polyethylene part to have an original appearance, your only option will be to buy a new part. If you can live with the as-welded appearance, then don't worry about painting the part at all.

If, for some reason, you insist on trying to paint a polyethylene part, use the same basic procedures as described in the previous section for unpainted TPOs. Clean the part very well with an abrasive plastic prep soap. Clean with a plastic cleaning solution. Then apply an adhesion promoter before the color coat.

The color coat should be flexible and resistant to gasoline. A single-stage catalyzed urethane paint should give the best results. Whatever kind of paint is used, the refinished part won't have the same semi-translucent appearance of the original part. Furthermore, the paint is not likely to be able to stand up to the abuse that dirt bikes regularly receive. If the fender is flexed or if rocks hit it, it is likely to crack or chip off.

Be forewarned that attempting to paint a polyethylene part may be an exercise in futility. Balance this factor against the cost of a new replacement part before you decide to go ahead with a repair.

Tools of the Trade

Beyond the normal hand tools that the typical handyman might have in his garage, there are a few specialized tools that are either essential or very nice to have for doing plastic repairs. Let's take a closer look at these specialized tools.

Heat Guns

High temperature heat guns are great for removing dents and distortions from damaged plastic. By heating the plastic thoroughly first, the distortions can be forced out by hand then quenched with water. These tools look like hair dryers, but they'll set your hair on fire if you use them for that purpose! They can put out air exceeding 1000 degrees F. Heat guns range in price from $100 to $200.

If you're working exclusively on street-bike fairings, you can probably get away without a heat gun as rigid plastics tend to shatter and break rather than distort. A heat gun would be nearly essential if you plan to do lots of TPO and urethane bumper cover repairs, however. These softer plastics tend to distort.

Die Grinders

Die grinders come in two styles: air and electric. Electric die grinders (such as the Dremel tool) are convenient and easy to use. They're great for tight areas and detail work. However, because their tools are rather small (1/8-inch-diameter shank), they tend to be slower when V-grooving larger areas.

Air die grinders do require a source of compressed air, so they're not quite as convenient as an electric die grinder. However, they use 1/4-inch shank tools and have correspondingly larger

cutting surfaces. These tools can hog out a large V-groove in very short order. In fact, if you've got a sharp carbide tip on your air die grinder, don't sneeze while grinding your V-groove as you're liable to bore a hole right through the plastic. Prices for die grinders range from $25 to $100.

Angle Drills

An angle drill is a tool that most handymen (and most bodymen, for that matter) don't have, but it's so useful that I'd strongly recommend it to

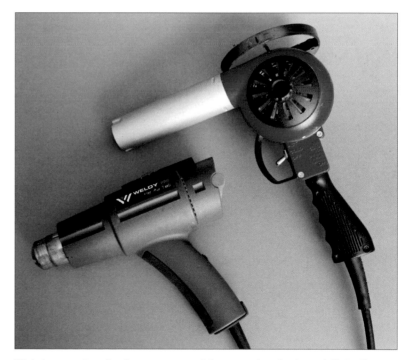

High temperature heat guns are great for removing dents and distortions from damaged plastic.

anyone who is considering doing more than just the occasional plastic repair. The angle drill is basically a variable-speed electric drill with its output shaft at 90 degrees from the motor. Chuck up a 3M Roloc disc holder and you're ready to grind any plastic. Electric grinders are much preferred to air grinders because they have high torque at low speed. The more common air grinder doesn't generate sufficient torque until the speed gets very high—speeds that will generate enough friction heat to melt many plastics. Get an electric angle drill. (Send your thank-you letters to me at the address shown in the front of this book!) Prices for high-quality angle drills range from $200 to $300.

Sanding Blocks

To get the best contour and optimum smoothness when sanding your cosmetic filler, nothing beats a good, flat sanding block and a bunch of elbow grease. Power sanders and DAs are great work-saving devices in the right hands, but they tend to move so quickly that they'll exaggerate mistakes before you know you've made one. Sanding by hand using a sanding block allows you to monitor the precise rate of material removal. You can also achieve a better match to the profile of the original part by sanding in an "X" pattern over the repair area. Small blocks take a fourth sheet of 9x12-inch paper. These are great for general purpose blocking. Fileboards take a special long and skinny sandpaper. These are great for rough contouring damage on flat or smoothly contoured parts. Prices for sanding blocks range from $5 to $25.

Electric die grinders (such as the Dremel tool) are convenient and easy to use. They're great for tight areas and detail work. Air die grinders require a source of compressed air, so they're not quite as convenient as an electric die grinder, but they have correspondingly larger cutting surfaces.

An angle drill is basically a variable-speed electric drill with its output shaft at 90 degrees from the motor. Electric grinders are much preferred to air grinders because they have high torque at low speed.

Dual Action, or DA, sanders have to be used with caution, but they are so useful it's hard to imagine doing any repair or refinishing job without one. Get the best one you can afford. Hook-and-loop type sandpaper is expensive, but much more convenient when you want to swap out grades of paper often.

Siphon guns draw their paint up from a cup positioned below the aerator tip. The movement of air within the gun creates a vacuum that draws the paint up through a tube. Siphon guns are no longer favored by professionals for spraying finish coats, but they are still used for for spraying primers and for other situations where the finish is not that important.

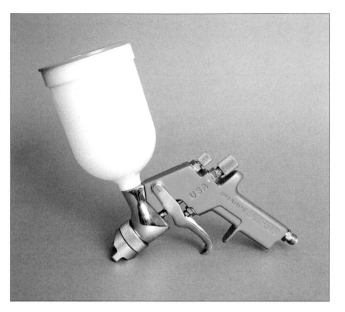

Gravity-feed guns are the most popular type of spray guns among professionals for doing fine-quality finish work. With the paint gun above the aerator tip, the paint will flow out naturally, making it easier for the gun to spray higher-viscosity fluids.

Dual Action Sanders

Dual Action, or DA, sanders have to be used with caution, but they are so useful it's hard to imagine doing any repair or refinishing job without one. Prices for DAs can range from $40 to $300, but generally the more money you spend, the better the quality, the more durable, and the lighter the tool will be. Get the best one you can afford. Also, consider getting some of the hook-and-loop type sandpaper for it. It's more expensive, but much more convenient when you want to swap out grades of paper often.

Siphon-feed Spray Guns

There are two basic formats for spray guns: siphon- and gravity-feed. Siphon guns, such as these shown here, draw their paint up from a cup positioned below the aerator tip. The movement of air within the gun creates a vacuum that draws the paint up through a tube. Siphon guns are no longer favored by professionals for spraying finish coats, but they are still useful for do-it-yourselfers, especially because they tend to be

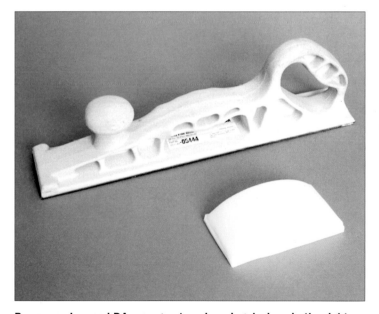

Power sanders and DAs are great work-saving devices in the right hands, but they tend to move so quickly that they'll exaggerate mistakes before you know you've made one. Sanding by hand using a sanding block allows you to monitor the precise rate of material removal. Small blocks work well for general purpose blocking. Fileboards are great for rough contouring damage on flat or smoothly contoured parts.

less expensive than gravity-feed guns. Professionals also use siphon guns for spraying primers and for other situations where the finish is not that important. Siphon spray guns typically range in price from $30 to $200.

Gravity-feed Spray Guns

Gravity-feed guns are the most popular type of spray guns among professionals for doing fine-quality finish work. With the paint gun above the aerator tip, the paint will flow out naturally, making it easier for the gun to spray higher-viscosity fluids. Prices of gravity-feed spray guns range from $100 to $500.

The Science of Adhesion

All of the repair and refinishing processes discussed in this book, except for fusion welding, involve the adhesion of a foreign material onto the plastic substrate to be repaired. Two-parts, hot-melts, cyanoacrylates, and methacrylates are what we call *adhesives,* but they themselves are plastic materials (thermoset or thermoplastic) with their own specific chemical makeup and molecular structure. Paint coatings are also plastic materials that are subject to the principles of adhesion.

In this book, I have discussed at length which type of adhesive works better for various substrates. In this appendix, I will briefly discuss the "whys and hows" of adhesives, in the hope that you will become more sensitive to the importance of cleaning the surface prior to the application of any coating.

Adhesive Bond Strength

The strength of an adhesive bond is a phenomenon that occurs at the molecular level between atoms of the substrate and the adhesive over very short distances (on the order of 1×10^{-9} in). It is a very complex phenomenon related to physical effects and chemical reactions at the interface between adhesive and substrate.

There are two elements of an adhesive bond: *cohesion* and *adhesion.* Cohesion is associated with the strength of the bond among the molecules of the adhesive itself. Adhesion is related to the strength of the bond between the adhesive and the substrate.

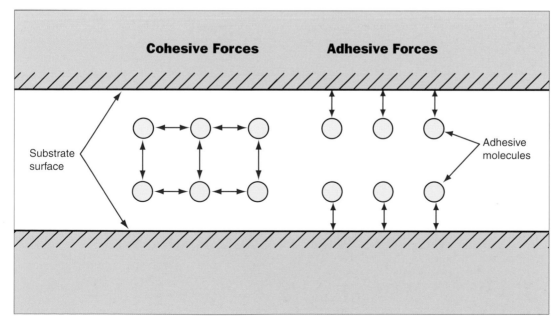

Cohesion is associated with the strength of the bond among the molecules of the adhesive itself.

Adhesion is related to the strength of the bond between the adhesive and the substrate.

If an adhesive joint fails, it may suffer a cohesive failure, an adhesive failure, or some combination of the two. A cohesive failure occurs when the adhesive itself tears apart, leaving the adhesive on both surfaces. Conversely, adhesive failure occurs when the adhesive tears clean away from one of the substrates. Interestingly, adhesion itself cannot be defined except under a situation of destructive deformation, i.e., you can't determine adhesion until you tear the adhesive joint apart.

On plastics substrates, we're mainly concerned about adhesive failure. The main problem with plastic substrates is low surface energy. This inhibits the adhesive from wetting out on the surface and thus coming into close physical contact with the substrate.

There are three main things necessary for a good adhesive bond on plastic substrates:

- Wetting of the surface by the adhesive or coating
- Cleanliness of the surface
- Surface preparation

Table B.1 - Surface Energy of Various Materials	
Material	**Surface Tension (dynes/cm)**
Copper	1000
Aluminum	500
Water	73
Epoxy resin	47
Polycarbonate	46
Polyester resin	43
ABS	35
Polyethylene	30
Teflon	18

Wetting of the Surface

In order to obtain an interaction between the adhesive and the substrate, it is necessary for the adhesive to wet the substrate. Since the phenomenon of adhesion occurs over such short distances, if the adhesive does not wet out and get into all the little nooks and crannies in the substrate's surface, adhesion simply cannot take place.

On plastic substrates, low surface energy inhibits the adhesive from wetting out on the surface and thus coming into close physical contact with it. If the adhesive does not get into all the little nooks and crannies in the substrate's surface, adhesion simply cannot take place. If the liquid has a lower surface energy than the substrate, the liquid will wet out on the surface.

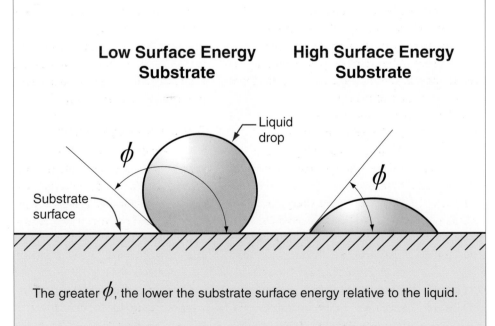

The greater ϕ, the lower the substrate surface energy relative to the liquid.

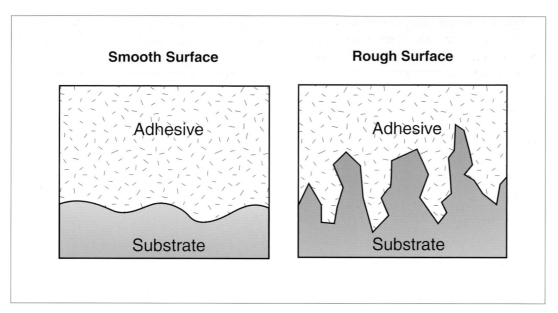

Smooth Surface

Adhesive

Substrate

Rough Surface

Adhesive

Substrate

If greatly magnified, the total area of the rough surface is much greater than that of the smooth surface, despite the fact that their gross dimensions are identical. This increase in surface area and roughness increases the molecular bonding forces between the adhesive and substrate and also provides for some mechanical interlocking.

Surface wetting is mainly a function of the relative surface energy of both the substrate and the adhesive in liquid state. If the liquid has a lower surface energy than the substrate, the liquid will wet out on the surface.

A good example of this phenomenon in action is how water beads up and rolls off the surface of a freshly waxed car. Because the wax has a low surface energy, the water droplets would rather stick to themselves via surface tension than wet out on the surface of the car.

If the surface is not waxed, the water will sheet out and wet the paint. In this case, the surface energy of the painted car is higher than the surface tension of the water, so the water flows out and wets the surface.

Table B.1 shows the surface energy of a few common metals and plastics to give you an idea of why some plastics are more difficult to adhere to than others. As you can see, the surface energy of epoxy resin is higher than that of most plastics, especially polyethylene. This is the reason good surface preparation, cleanliness, and the use of an adhesion promoting coating are often important when making plastic repairs.

Surface Cleanliness

As often happens in repair work, the broken part in question has been in service for some time and subjected to the environment. The surface will have a variety of contaminants on it, but the ones you should be most concerned about are petroleum-based contaminants, like motor oil and gasoline. Such contaminants have a surface energy even lower than that of most plastics, so you definitely don't want to have that on the surface to further reduce adhesion.

Surface Preparation

If you looked at a cross section of the surface of a properly prepared substrate through an electron microscope (to get down to the scale of the distances over which adhesion takes place), it might have the appearance of the Himalayan mountains. There would be huge mountains and valleys into which the atoms of the adhesive could settle themselves.

The nooks and crannies in the surface provide an opportunity for the adhesive to *lock in* to the surface mechanically, so the bond strength can rely not only on the adhesive strength of the bond but on the cohesive strength of the adhesive as well.

Furthermore, a roughed-up surface provides a much greater total surface area than a smooth one with the same gross dimensions. The strength of the bond is proportional to the total surface area over which the adhesive is applied, so a rough surface is much preferred to a smooth one. That's why I strongly suggest sand-scratching any glossy areas with coarse sandpaper before applying any type of adhesive.

Resource Directory

To varying degrees, all the manufacturers of plastic repair products provide information about and training on their products. The best source of the latest information would be at the respective manufacturer's website. Web addresses are listed in Appendix D.

The collision industry training association, I-CAR, provides an excellent course on plastic repair, among other things. Information on their curriculum is available at their website, www.i-car.com, or through their toll-free number, 1-888-I-CAR-USA.

Plastic Repair Manufacturers

International Epoxies and Sealants
6330 118th Avenue N
Largo, FL 34643
www.internationalepoxies.com
813-546-8923, 1-800-451-7206

SEM Products
651 Michael Wylie Dr.
Charlotte, NC 28217
www.semproducts.com
704-522-1006, 1-800-831-1122

Dominion Sure Seal
6175 Danville Rd.
Mississauga, ON L5T 2H7 Canada
www.dominionsureseal.com
216-656-5008

Duramix
1630 Fiske Place
Oxnard, CA 93033
www.duramix.com
805-483-2043, 1-800-537-9204

Lord Fusor
2000 W. Grandview Blvd.
Erie, PA 16514-0038
www.fusor.com
814-868-3611

Plastex
2855 Ravazza Rd
Reno, NV 89511
www.plastex.net
702-852-4066

Plast-Aid
PO Box 2156
Estes Park, CO 80517
www.plast-aid.com
970-577-1000

ProForm
430 Harrop Drive
Milton, ON L9T 3H2 Canada
905-878-4990

ProTech
425 Berry Street
Winnipeg, MB R3L 1N6 CANADA
www.protechnology.com
204-988-3484

Rubber Seal Products
5751 N Webster St.
Dayton, OH 45414
http://www.rubber-seal.com
513-890-6547, 1-800-257-6547

Transtar
2040 Heiserman Drive
Brighton, MI 48116
http://www.tat-co.com
810-220-3000, 1-800-824-2843

U.S. Chemical & Plastics
P.O. Box 709
600 Nova Dr. SE
Massillon, OH 44648-0709
www.uschem.com
330-830-6000, 1-800-321-0672

Urethane Supply Company
1128 Kirk Rd
Rainsville, AL 35986
www.urethanesupply.com
256-638-4103, 800-633-3047

Crest Industries, Inc.
3841 13th Street
Wyandotte, MI 48192
www.crestauto.com
313-283-4100, 1-800-822-4100

Bondo Mar-Hyde
2628 Pearl Rd.
Medina, OH 44258
www.bondomarhyde.com
1-800-421-2663

3M Automotive Aftermarket Division
www.3m.com
1-888-3M-HELPS

Wurth Canada, Ltd.
6330 Tomken Road
Mississauga ON L5T 1N2 Canada
www.wurthcanada.com
905-564-6225, 1-800-263-5002

Bibliography

Charrier, Jean-Michel. *Polymeric Materials and Processing: Plastics, Elastomers, and Composites.* Hanser Publishers, 1990.

Baghdachi, Jamil. *Adhesives Bonding Technology.* Seminar Notes Published by Society of Automotive Engineers, Course No. 90023, 1994.

Braun, Deitrich. *Simple Methods for Identification of Plastics.* Second edition. Hanser Publishers, 1986.

Brydson, J.A. *Plastics Materials.* Third edition. Whitefriars Press Ltd., 1975.

Woebcken, Wilbrand. *International Plastics Handbook for the Technologist, Engineer, and User.* Third edition. Hanser Publishers, 1995.

New Developments in Exterior Body Panels and Bumper Systems. Society of Automotive Engineers, Inc., 1991. SAE Publication No. SP-859.

Plastics Digest. Published by D.A.T.A., a division of Information Handling Services, Inc.

Plastics in Automobile Bumper Systems and Exterior Panels. Society of Automotive Engineers, Inc., 1990. SAE Publication No. SP-821.

Plastics in Automobile Instrument Panels, Trim and Seating. Society of Automotive Engineers, Inc., 1990. SAE Publication No. SP-822.

Plastics in Automobiles: Bumper Systems, Interior Trim, Instrument Panels, and Exterior Panels. Society of Automotive Engineers, Inc., 1989. SAE Publication No. SP-772.

Plastics in Automotive Applications: An Overview. Edited by Geaman, Phelps, and Rusch. Society of Automotive Engineers, Inc., 1988. SAE Publication No. PT-32.

Index

About the Author

Kurt Lammon is president of Urethane Supply Company, a manufacturer of plastic repair and refinishing products for the automotive collision repair industry. At Urethane Supply Company, he has served in the roles of technical support and new product development since 1995. His duties in product development and customer support require almost daily use of Urethane Supply's and competitors' products in repairing and refinishing a wide range of automotive, motorcycle, and recreational vehicle plastics.

Lammon was a member of the change board selected by I-CAR for revisions done to their plastic repair course in 1999. He has made hundreds of presentations on the subject of plastic repair to insurance industry professionals and technicians in the auto collision repair industry in a variety of venues, and has received instructor-level training from I-CAR.

Prior to his experience at Urethane Supply Company, Lammon spent five years at Allied Signal Corporation as a design and test engineer on the ATF3 turbofan engine, gaining him great exposure to high-tech materials and manufacturing methods. He has a BS in Mechanical Engineering with a minor in Materials Science from the University of Florida and an MS in Industrial Administration from Carnegie Mellon University. He is a member of the Society of Automotive Engineers.

Other Tech Series Titles by
Whitehorse Press
the motorcycle information company

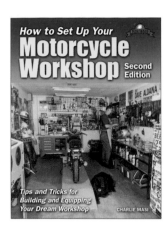

Softbound
8¼ x 10½ inches
160 pages
Approx. 200 b/w illus.

ISBN: 1-884313-43-4
Order Code: MASI2
Price: $19.95

How to Set Up Your Motorcycle Workshop - 2nd Ed.

by Charlie Masi

Everything you need to know about designing, building, and equipping a workshop, with practical information that will help you make the most of your space and budget. New edition includes profiles of real-world workshops, from small garage spaces to purpose-built restoration and race-prep shops.

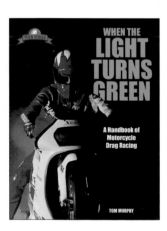

Softbound
8¼ x 10½ inches
176 pages
Approx. 300 b/w illus.

ISBN: 1-884313-29-9
Order Code: WLTG
Price: $19.95

When the Light Turns Green:
A Handbook of Motorcycle Drag Racing

by Tom Murphy

From engines, carburetors, and fuel injectors to ignition systems and clutches, this is a complete guide on how to build and operate a drag machine, with tips to help you prepare mentally for drag racing, as well as an illustrated course in racing techniques, correct form, and positioning.

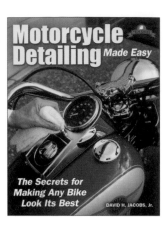

Softbound
8¼ x 10½ inches
144 pages
Approx. 300 b/w illus.

ISBN: 1-884313-35-3
Order Code: MDME
Price: $19.95

Motorcycle Detailing Made Easy

by David H. Jacobs, Jr.

Whether you want to return your bike to showroom condition, get it ready to sell, or prepare it for a custom show, this book will teach you what cleaning a motorcycle is all about. Learn the tricks that will help you keep your bike looking great.

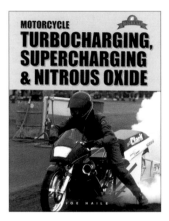

Softbound
8¼ x 10½ inches
198 pages
Approx. 280 b/w illus.

ISBN: 1-884313-07-8
Order Code: HAIL
Price: $19.95

Motorcycle Turbocharging,
Supercharging & Nitrous Oxide

by Joe Haile

Written by the master himself, this book will give you a thorough understanding of the principles of forced induction systems and the practical matters involved in putting these principles to work to boost power. Helpful tips on what equipment to buy, how to use it, and much more.